The School Administrator's Guide for Supporting Students from Military Families

Ron Avi Astor,
Linda Jacobson, Rami Benbenishty
Hazel R. Atuel, Tamika Gilreath, Marleen Wong,
Kris M. Tunac De Pedro, Monica Christina Esqueda,
and Joey Nuñez Estrada Jr.

Teachers College
Columbia University
New York and London

Military Child Education Coalition®
909 Mountain Lion Circle
Harker Heights, TX 76548

This publication was developed by the USC Building Capacity in Military Connected Schools team, in part, with grant funds from the U.S. Department of Defense Education Activity under Award Number HE1254-10-1-0041. The views expressed in this profile do not necessarily reflect the positions or policies of the Department, and no official endorsement by the Department is intended or should be inferred.

All royalties from the sale of this book are being donated to military children's educational causes.

Published simultaneously by Teachers College Press, 1234 Amsterdam Avenue, New York, NY 10027 and by the Military Child Education Coalition®, 909 Mountain Lion Circle, Harker Heights, Texas 76548

Library of Congress Cataloging-in-Publication Data

The school administrator's guide for supporting students from military families /
  Ron Avi Astor ... [et al.].
    p. cm.
  Includes bibliographical references and index.
  ISBN 978-0-8077-5370-5 (pbk. : alk. paper)
    1. Children of military personnel–Education–United States. 2. School
  management and organization–United States. I. Astor, Ron Avi.
  LC5081.S36 2012
  379.1'21–dc23   2012020713

ISBN 978-0-8077-5370-5 (paperback)

Printed on acid-free paper
Manufactured in the United States of America

19   18   17   16   15   14   13   12   8   7   6   5   4   3   2   1

Contents

Preface

As we were writing this book, the war in Iraq officially ended, and a date has been set for withdrawing troops from Afghanistan.

Public support for successful reunions between U.S. service members and their families should be strong, so that our men and women in uniform can make smooth transitions to life back at home. Some parents returning from deployments will be looking for new careers in the face of "downsizing," while others will be training for future assignments overseas. These can be stressful times for military families.

Public schools can potentially provide a setting in which children can feel a sense of security. A "bedrock." "A consistent, safe place." Those are the words one principal we talked to used to describe what school should be for children in military families, "no matter what is going on at home, no matter where you are in the deployment cycle."

We have worked with many military-connected school districts in developing this guide. On a regular basis, we heard stories of how resilient military children are—able to quickly adjust to new schools, new friends, and shifting academic demands. And we've witnessed the love and professionalism in these supportive public schools.

But resiliency isn't necessarily an inborn trait. These fantastic schools are fostering strength, courage, and a sense of pride in these students. They honor and celebrate the many layers of sacrifices made by these families. They are making sure a friendly face is there to greet students when they enroll. They are giving them opportunities to talk about the places they have lived. And they are hiring professionals trained to respond during tough times, so children—many of whom have had to take on adult responsibilities in their homes while a parent is away—can focus on being students.

In searching across the country for good ideas, evidence-supported practices, and grassroots efforts, we've learned that school communities can help to relieve some of the stress on military families. Great schools can help military students and families thrive, provide an extra sense of connectedness, and lend a helping hand when needed.

Schools have generated creative ideas to welcome military children. For example, one school created a friendship garden so military children could literally, and figuratively, put down some roots in their new school and feel more connected.

When another school asked military children to serve as "tour guides" and buddies to incoming students, the transition period went much more smoothly and parents felt less anxious about their children's first days in a new place. And others hosted morning coffee chats for military parents so they could get better acquainted and share ideas for supporting each other.

These are simple practices—but they are practices that can be implemented by any school, and that can create positive experiences for children who move an average of nine times before they graduate from high school.

This book was created by a diverse team of professionals at the University of Southern California. Our research included hours of interviews with military families, model school principals, excellent teachers, and military school liaison officers, as well as observations of programs that are working well. We also carefully integrated research, reviewed the literature, searched the Internet, and explored the work of national organizations in selecting the most beneficial practices, programs, and resources to present.

Our deepest hope is that this book provides you with scientifically sound, practical, and eye-opening ideas for making military families feel more welcome and supported in public schools. We hope civilians will recognize that military culture is an important diversity group to include in curriculum and school climate reform. Ultimately, caring, supportive, culturally appropriate, and thoughtful school environments could radically change the lives of all students, but even more so for those who have endured so much.

All of the royalties from the sale of this book are being donated to non-profit, education-oriented organizations benefitting military children.

Acknowledgments

This guide seeks to make public schools more supportive of military families. We first want to thank the military families who have sacrificed so much for our country. We thank you for your contributions to our society and to our world. Military families and children are strong, proud, and resilient. We saw and heard this every place we went. Many of the ideas generated in this guide originated from educators who themselves had a military family member or who have served. We thank them for their continued commitment.

The authors wish to sincerely thank the many citizens and professionals in school districts, government, the military, and in nonprofit organizations who have shared their best practices so we could include them in this guide. We especially want to thank the school liaison officers from all branches of the military who work tirelessly to improve school experiences for military children.

To all the district officials, principals, assistant principals, teachers, pupil personnel, parents, and students: thank you for sharing with us your ideas, stories, and photos so that other schools can learn how to make military children feel more welcome and appreciated. Our partners at San Diego State University, UC San Diego, and the University of California Los Angeles have also been instrumental in elevating this work to a regional level. The over 100 master's and doctoral students in social work and education from USC, as well as the master's students in social work, school counseling, and school psychology from SDSU, also deserve special recognition for inspiring many of the recommendations in this book. We thank the undergraduate students in the Partners at Learning program at UCSD.

Many scientific experts and research organizations have advised us through the process of creating this guide, including the members of our International Advisory Board, various educational consultants, the Military Family Research Institute, the National Military Family Association, and the Department of Defense Education Activity (DoDEA).

In particular, we would like to thank: the DoDEA partnership program for national leadership, excellent materials and programs, and vigilant dissemination of best practices to public schools; the Military Child Education Coalition for educating teachers, counselors, parents, and administrators; the American Association of Colleges of Teacher Education for engaging university schools of education; and most importantly, the University of Southern California (USC) schools of social work and education, the Center for Research and Innovation on Veterans and Military Families, and Hamovitch Research Center for their commitment to train professionals in university settings to work with military families. We also want to recognize Dr. Jill Biden, Michelle Obama, and their staffs for support and for nationally prioritizing the needs of military children and families. Their Joining Forces campaign highlights the need to educate universities and public schools about the needs of military students.

Introduction

> Schools with large numbers of military dependents can benefit greatly by understanding not only the military culture but also the significant and unprecedented dynamics created by the current status of our nation's military. When schools embrace their families' challenges, and honor the exceptionality of their students and their parents, they serve our littlest heroes and foster their academic success.
>
> —Pat Kurtz, Principal,
> Santa Margarita Elementary School, Oceanside, California

As a principal, you are the primary leader in charge of determining the mission and climate of your school. The policies and procedures followed by your teachers and staff create the first—and often lasting—impressions that students and their parents receive when they become part of your school.

Those practices can have a significant impact on one group of students that haven't received much attention from educators—military children. The frequency with which these students move between schools and face stressful family situations can make it challenging for them to feel part of a school community and can hinder their academic progress and emotional health.

Creating a welcoming environment in your school that is sensitive to the needs of military families can help to provide stability for students who must face many transitions in their lives.

Children who are born into military families live unique and interesting lives. They have opportunities to travel around the world, to gain firsthand knowledge of cultures that most American students only read about, and can often adapt quickly to new situations and surroundings. But they also face significant challenges and have special circumstances that civilian children and families don't experience. These can include gaps in school attendance and learning, being separated from a parent who has been deployed, and a sense of isolation in the midst of a civilian community that cannot relate to the obstacles and challenges they face.

In the drive to improve schools, education reformers have focused mainly on the learning needs of minority students, students with disabilities, English learners, and even preschool-age children. But they have rarely considered the academic and social needs of students from military families.

In your administrator preparation, you probably were not trained to recognize the unique circumstances and challenges that children face when they grow up in a military family. And schools, by and large, have not created environments in which military children feel welcomed and supported.

One explanation for this gap in knowledge and practice could be that many educators and even policymakers have the misconception that all service members' children live on bases and attend Department of Defense Education Activity (DoDEA) schools. In fact, even many education researchers tend to make generalizations about military children based on findings that pertain only to students who attend schools and preschools operated by the DoDEA.

In reality, only about 7% of U.S. military children—about 86,000—attend schools and preschools operated by DoDEA. These schools—located both in the States and on bases overseas—have staff that are trained and prepared to respond to the needs of military children and families. But the *vast majority* of military children attend regular public schools with staff that may or may not be familiar with or sensitive to the realities of military life, such as frequent moves and the deployment of a parent. Your school might be considered "military-connected" because, according to the government's definition, at least 3% of your students have parents in the military. Or, you may just have a few students from military families. Either way, this guide can inform you about the challenges they face and suggest ways to make their time in your school as positive and productive as possible.

There are also more than a million students whose parents are in the National Guard and Reserves. These students live typical civilian lives, but when their parents' units are called into action, they are suddenly thrust into an unfamiliar military lifestyle. These students may also require special attention and understanding in your school. Research finds that their parents are less likely to have access to or use support services offered by the military.

It might also be helpful for you to realize that because military members are often young, you may have a student who has an older brother or sister who is deployed. And because of the heavy involvement of the Guard and Reserves in Iraq and Afghanistan, some children have grandparents that have been deployed.

Many military students often feel misunderstood in the schools they attend, and you may lack the knowledge and resources you need to make your school more welcoming to military children and families. There are, however, some districts and schools that perform a remarkable job working with military families. The practices and programs they have implemented need to be shared so that all schools serving military children are better equipped to include these families and respond to their concerns.

If your school serves military students, it is critical that you become more aware of this population and acquire strategies to support both their academic and social-emotional development. Organizations such as the Military Child Education Coalition, for example, have created popular workshops and materials focused on education issues related to military families. There are very few evidence-based programs, however, aimed at creating a more military-friendly culture in civilian schools.

DESCRIPTION OF THIS GUIDE

The goal of this resource guide is to create a clearinghouse of ideas and promising practices that have been generated by educators working within military-connected schools. Part of a 4-year project called "Building Capacity to Create Highly Supportive Military-Connected School Districts," this guide is a groundbreaking effort to bring educators into the conversation about how to make schools more inviting and supportive for this unique group of students. The project, created by a grant from DoDEA to a consortium of eight school districts and the University of Southern California, is focused on improving school climate so that the education community is more welcoming to military children. Our goal is to give educators strategies to support these students' academic progress and social and emotional well-being, and to encourage all school staff members to recognize the sacrifices that military children make because of their parents' service.

In addition to this guide, we have also written companion versions for pupil personnel, teachers, and military parents. You can inform people in those roles about the guides that are appropriate for them.

The lives of military children are receiving attention at the highest levels of government. A 2011 presidential initiative boosted efforts across all federal agencies to support military families—a focus that is expected to continue in future administrations.

In addition, the Department of Defense and the Department of Education have agreed that supporting military children in civilian schools should be a high priority, and that traditional public and private schools and DoDEA schools should begin sharing information about successful practices and policies.

This guide will:

- inform you about many of the recurring issues military students may face, such as school mobility, family stress created by a parent's deployment or return home, and exposure to trauma.

- highlight many of those practices, strategies, and policies that you can use to make your school more welcoming for military families and support students' academic and social-emotional needs.
- refer you to organizations and services you can use as resources to learn more about the concerns of military children and families. *Special Note: We have listed website links for all of the resources that we have included, but we realize that links change or disappear. Search online for the organizations or names of articles if a link no longer works.*
- draw attention to opportunities for further research and policy issues that could improve the way schools serve military students.

THE ISSUE OF TRANSITION

When a child grows up with one or both parents in the armed services, it's inevitable that he or she will change schools much more often than nonmilitary students. For example, almost 12% of military students in secondary schools told us that they have changed schools three times in the past 5 years. As a principal, you are aware that frequent moves can interrupt academic progress and hinder a student's social relationships.

But the life of a military child is an ongoing series of transitions that take place even when an actual relocation is not involved. This is important for you to keep in mind, so transition is a theme that will cut across all topics addressed in this guide.

Every time a parent is deployed or returns from an assignment ("reintegration") is a disruption that can lead to changing roles in the family structure and routine or changing relationships with parents.

Simply being "the new kid" in school is not the only time a military child may become distracted by the shifting nature of his or her home environment. Making new students feel welcome is one responsibility that schools have, but it is also important to provide ongoing support for military students in the school setting.

"[Children] need something that they can rely on that's consistent, especially with multiple deployments," says Diana Ashe, a mother, a former Marine, and the wife of a Marine. She also holds a Master's of Social Work from USC. "The more constant structure you can have within a school and everybody working within a community and as a group, the better off the kids will be."

It is our hope that this guide gives you the knowledge and resources you need to create a highly supportive military-connected school.

CHAPTER 1

An Introduction to Military Culture

To best serve the military children and families in your school, it's useful to first understand their unique lifestyle. Currently, less than 1% of the population serves in the military. As a result, many members of civilian society are unfamiliar with military culture. Military culture, much like any culture, "is comprised of values, beliefs, traditions, and norms that govern the social behavior of service members," write Herbert Exum, Jose Coll, and Eugenia Weiss in their 2011 book *A Civilian Primer for Counseling Military Veterans* (p. 17).

These authors, having many years of service in the military and working with military families, say that such values, beliefs, traditions, and norms determine how members of the military and veterans conduct themselves from "the moment they enter [into] military [service]" (p. 19). Though values may differ, to a degree, by branch, "honor, courage, loyalty, integrity, and commitment" are held in high esteem across all military branches (p. 17).

Even as you read this chapter, however, remember not to make generalizations about military students. Even though military families share cultural characteristics due to their military affiliation, each family has other characteristics–ethnicity, socioeconomic status, past experiences in public schools, etc.–that also shape their opinions and actions.

CODES OF CONDUCT

Just as norms and laws dictate behavior within civilian societies and cultures, standards of conduct govern how service members think and act, write Exum and colleagues. Remaining committed to these standards is considered critical to the mission and success of the armed forces. Following the chain of command is among the most significant codes of conduct. In their book, Exum and colleagues cite World War II veteran Willard Waller, who in 1944 wrote:

chain of command refers to the succession of commanding officers from superior to subordinate through which command is exercised via orders. [The chain of command] settles all questions of authority and avoids clashes of personality through a hierarchal system in which everyone has a place in relation to the other. Orders come from the top down and never from the bottom up. Everyone is under orders and there can never be any doubt regarding who has the right to order whom to do what (p. 21).

Continuing on the topic, Exum and colleagues wrote that the hierarchal nature of the chain of command ensures that

social status in the military is very clear, whereby officers have higher status than enlisted personnel and both officers and enlisted personnel are further ordered in status according to rank. Duties, responsibilities, pay, living arrangements, and social interactions are all determined by rank, and appropriate insignia displayed on the military uniform easily identifies rank. Superiors and subordinates are clearly delineated, and one's place in the social structure is never ambiguous (p. 24).

As a school administrator, you might find that military parents expect your school (and perhaps your parent organization) to function in the same way. They might not be open to advice or direction from a teacher or counselor and may instead demand your approval of any decision involving their children. Furthermore, they may expect you to "discipline" your staff, similar to the way issues are handled by the military command.

MILITARY FAMILIES

Of the 2.2 million individuals serving in active, National Guard, or Reserve units in 2009, approximately 55% were married and 40% had at least two children, notes Major Eric Flake, a physician at Madigan Army Medical Center. The number of dual-career couples in which both parents are serving active duty is also increasing, historian Anni Baker noted in 2008.

These families—including the children—share a unique cultural context. Similar to their loved ones serving in uniform, military culture exerts "normative pressures on the behavior of [military children and their families]. Family members informally carry the rank of the service member, and behavioral prescriptions vary accordingly," wrote University of Maryland sociologist Mady W. Segal in a 1989 article, "The Nature of Work and Family Linkages: A Theoretical Perspective" (pp. 23–24). Baker emphasized that "on or off base, there is great pressure to conform to common standards of behavior." And, according to Segal, failure to do so may negatively impact their loved one's career goals.

SEEKING HELP

Within the military, problems are addressed according to the chain of command. Depending on the severity of the issue and how it might be perceived, a service member may be hesitant to report or seek help for individual problems. Service members may be reluctant to report individual health problems, especially mental health issues. Military culture has traditionally viewed mental illness as a sign of weakness, but this is a perception that the military is working to change. Nevertheless, signs of psychological illness may result in the service member being "perceived as unfit for duty" or worse yet, a security risk, thus limiting opportunities for career advancement, Exum and colleagues write. For these reasons, service members may sometimes not seek help.

This characteristic may affect how the family interacts with the staff at your school. Mindful that their behavior is subject to scrutiny and may negatively impact their loved one's career, members of military families may be reluctant to seek help. Therefore, military children who are struggling academically and/or emotionally may not be able to access necessary supports. Asking for help would draw unwanted attention to the family and service member.

Military family members may also worry that their child's problem will be perceived as a sign of weakness, Segal noted. To effectively support military families and children in need, schools must first understand the unique cultural contexts of military families. Military parents may also be resistant to interventions that target specific children since this approach would contradict the military's emphasis on groups over individuals. Support services and interventions may be more effective if delivered within a group setting. Any offer to help the child should be accompanied by respect. Supports must also *empower* military families with the strength and skills they need to make it through difficult times, psychology professor Charles Figley, now at Tulane University, wrote in his 1993 chapter, "Weathering the Storm at Home: War-Related Family Stress and Coping."

WHEN WORLDS COLLIDE:
CONTRASTING MILITARY AND CIVILIAN CULTURES

In addition to different attitudes toward seeking help, there are other ways in which the military families in your school may differ from nonmilitary families. Individuals who serve in the military form a distinct cultural group. Unlike U.S. civilian culture, which emphasizes individuality and personal freedom, military culture imposes "a strict hierarchal structure" that is "mission" focused, Exum and colleagues write (p. 24). Following the chain of command, obeying orders, and group solidarity are critical to fulfilling the mission. Given the pervasive nature of military culture, service members may be less comfortable interacting with civilians who are unfamiliar with military culture. The majority of service members, however, "are compelled to live in" civilian residential communities for a significant proportion of their career, Roger W. Little wrote in the 1971 *Handbook of Military Institutions.*

Therefore, service members and their families spend a substantial amount of time surrounded by civilian culture. The service member's interactions and participation in civilian culture, however, require adaptation that extends beyond simply removing one's uniform. Service members must navigate the norms, cultural codes, and social behaviors of civilians, such as public school staff. Tensions may therefore arise if the service member, or civilian, is unable to reconcile cultural differences, Exum and his co-authors write.

BENEFITS OF MILITARY SERVICE

While a number of demands are placed on military families, there are also a number of advantages that accompany military life. Lindsay Paden and Laurence Pezor emphasized this aspect in their 1993 article, "Uniforms and Youth: The Military Child and His or Her Family." "The opportunity to travel, to see different parts of the world and [to engage with] a variety of cultures," is unique, they write (p. 11). And instead of leading to problems, adversity in military families can provide opportunities for children to mature. Finally, given their collective circumstances, military families share an identity and bond that has endured over time, write Paden and Pezor.

It's clear that military culture is fundamentally different from civilian culture. Recognizing this fact and making an effort to understand military families' values, beliefs, traditions, and social norms can help schools better serve military children.

GLOSSARY OF TERMS

The education field is filled with jargon, acronyms, and terms that non-educators in your school may not understand. Likewise, the military has its own "language" that civilians may not know other than what they have heard on television or in the movies. Becoming familiar with many of these terms can help you become more informed about the military families in your school.

Active Duty: continuous duty on a daily basis; comparable to the civilian term "full-time employment."

Promising Practice Spotlight

The birth of the U.S. Marine Corps is celebrated each year with a cake-cutting ceremony in which the first slice is given to the oldest Marine present, who then hands it to the youngest Marine. The ritual represents the passing of knowledge and experience from older Marines to the next generation.

Students at Jefferson Middle School, located on the Camp Pendleton Marine Corps Base, shared in that tradition when the Marine Corps celebrated its 235th birthday on November 10, 2010. The ceremony illustrates what schools serving military students can do to integrate a military-themed ritual into the school day and make it relevant for all students.

Kim Becker, then a student in the USC School of Social Work—who specializes in military social work and was completing her internship at Jefferson—organized the event as an effort to recognize students at the school whose parents serve in the Marines. The ceremony was also intended to create more awareness among nonmilitary students.

"I wanted to allow all children to be exposed to the military culture, cause, and traditions," Becker, a Marine wife, told the *San Diego Union-Tribune*. "I also wanted to help military students here feel a sense of belonging, and create community cohesion between the base and the school."

Chris Hurst, the school's principal and a former Marine, used the event as an opportunity to encourage students to pursue excellence both in and out of school.

"Military children were acknowledged for their resiliency and culture," Becker wrote in her summary of the event, adding that she "hopes to see this project replicated within all military-impacted schools as a way to educate students and teachers about the military culture and lifestyle."

Schools serving students whose parents are in other branches of the military might want to find out which ceremonies would be appropriate to replicate in those communities.

Typical Marine birthday cake

BAH: Basic Allowance for Housing. Monthly housing assistance provided to service members who live off the military installation or in private housing on the installation.

Battalion: a unit of 300–1,000 soldiers under the command of a lieutenant colonel.

Brigade: a unit of 3,000–5,000 soldiers under the command of a colonel.

Care Package: a package sent from home containing food and/or personal items.

Chain of Command: the succession of commanding officers from a superior to a subordinate through which commands are executed; also the organizational structure of a branch of the armed forces: squad, platoon, company, battalion, brigade, division, corps, and army.

CO: Commanding Officer.

Company: a unit of 62–190 soldiers led by a captain.

Corps: the Marine Corps; also a unit of 20,000–40,000 soldiers under the command of a lieutenant general.

DoDDS: Department of Defense Dependent Schools. Schools operated in the United States and overseas by the Department of Defense Education Activity (DoDEA).

Dependent: a family member for whom a service member is legally and financially responsible–usually a spouse or child.

Deploy: to systematically station military persons or forces over an area; also the movement of forces within an area of military operation; the positioning of forces in a formation for battle. The term refers to military personnel being on temporary assignment away from their home base over an extended period of time.

Division: a unit of 10,000–15,000 soldiers under the command of a major general.

Inactive Reserve: affiliation with the military in a nontraining, nonpaying status after completing the minimum obligation of active duty service.

IED: Improvised Explosive Device.

Lifer: career military personnel.

MEPS: Military Entrance Processing Station. Military bases at various locations in the United States that receive and train new enlisted personnel.

MIA: Missing In Action.

MOS: Military Occupational Specialty.

NCO: Non-Commissioned Officer; an enlisted person ranked sergeant (E-4) or above.

Obligation: the period of time an individual agrees to serve on active duty, in the Reserves, or a combination of both.

OCS: Officer Candidate School. A program for college graduates with no prior military training that wish to become military officers. The program also accepts qualified enlisted personnel who wish to become officers.

Rank: Grade or official standing of commissioned and warrant officers.

Reserves: the military forces comprised of individuals who are not presently on full-time active duty but who may be called to active duty if needed.

R&R: rest and relaxation.

Sea Duty: an assignment (generally for 3 years) to any ship, whether or not scheduled for deployment, or to any aircraft squadron that may or may not be deployable; the term typically refers to Navy personnel.

Stand Down: a 3-day rest period for units coming out of the field.

Tour of Duty: a specified period of service obligation; also used to describe the location of a duty tour.

Sources: "Students at the Center," DoDEA (http://www.militaryk12partners. dodea.edu/studentsAtTheCenter/index.html); Exum et al., (2011)

FACTS AND FIGURES

Total Force Demographics (as of March 2011)

- Approximately 203,800 individuals are currently deployed (including Reservists and Guardsmen)
- Approximately 35% of the deployed force in Iraq and Afghanistan was comprised of Guardsmen and Reservists
- Approximately 200,000 women serve in the military

Casualties and Wounded (as of July 2011)

- Operation Iraqi Freedom (3/19/03–8/31/10): 4,421 casualties; 31,922 wounded
- Operation New Dawn (began 9/1/01): 56 casualties; 224 wounded
- Operation Enduring Freedom (began 10/7/01): 1,647 casualties; 12,450 wounded
- Traumatic Brain Injuries: 212,742 (total since 2000, as of March 2011)

Sources:

- Coll, J., Hassan, A., Rank, M., Reyes, V. A., & Wildy, M. (2011). Military culture [PowerPoint presentation]. University of Southern California.
- Defense and Veterans Brain Injury Center. (2011). *Traumatic brain injury: Numbers.* Available at: http://dvbic.org/TBI-Numbers.aspx
- U.S. Department of Defense. (2011). *Military personnel statistics.* Available at: http://siadapp.dmdc.osd.mil/personnel/MILITARY/miltop.htm
- U.S. Department of Defense. (2011). *News: Casualty status.* Available at: http://www.defense.gov/news/

CHAPTER 2

Mobility

As an experienced educator and school leader, you know that students who frequently change schools are less likely to perform well academically than those who are more stable. Highly transient students can fall behind in school because of missing days during a move or because of problems adjusting to new schools, classmates, and teachers. See our Research Highlights on Student Mobility at the end of this chapter.

Changing schools can contribute to children feeling sad, depressed, or angry, which can be displayed in a variety of ways, including poor behavior. Research findings on the social-emotional outcomes of frequent school transfers, however, are less conclusive than those on academic effects. Some children seem to grow more resilient with each move.

MOBILITY AND MILITARY CHILDREN

For children in military families, these mobility issues are compounded. They move three times more often than those in civilian families, and as a result can experience academic setbacks and other problems in schools. In addition, the school moves that military children experience may make the normal transitions that students encounter—such as the move from elementary to middle school or middle to high school—more troublesome than they would be for students who haven't experienced so many changes. As a

Key Points on Student Mobility

- Frequent school moves can cause students to fall behind academically and develop social/emotional problems.
- Mobility, however, doesn't affect every child the same way.
- Research provides insight into how mobility affects children in military families.
- School administrators can implement practices and provide resources that ease the stress and difficulty for students that come with changing schools.

> Many of the youngsters that come in as 3- and 4-year-olds, we'd find pretty quickly after placing them in programs, might have developmental disabilities that had never been picked up. If you move from community to community and don't stay anywhere too long and don't have an opportunity to form relationships and get to know families with other children, you don't really understand what normal child development is. So we've worked a lot with hooking those families up to different services in our community.
>
> —Nancy Kerwin, Executive Director, Student, Family, and Community Services, Chula Vista Elementary School District

principal, having many military students who frequently move in and out of your school creates many challenges. Your staff needs to be always ready to receive new students or help them move on to new schools. You may need to train your staff to handle these tasks and perhaps use creative strategies to ease the process. For instance, some schools have created "transition rooms," as the ones described later in this guide.

Research, however, suggests that the military lifestyle doesn't have to hinder students' chances of staying on top of their schoolwork or make them feel like outcasts in a new school. Some students may react positively to the experience because they get a chance to start over.

THE ROLE OF SCHOOLS

Your school can and should be part of a support network that assists students in making transitions between schools. You may not be able to control whether or not a child moves repeatedly, but there are strategies that your school can use to make new students feel welcome and in step with other students in the school, and to ease transitions for students leaving your school.

Education research cannot be generalized to the military student population. The knowledge that exists on student mobility tends to be based on other highly mobile groups, such as homeless students or children in foster care. While military children may have some needs in common with students in these groups, they should not be viewed with the same lens.

Even the practices recommended by some experts for reducing mobility—such as urging parents to avoid school changes—don't apply to military families. They don't have the option of refusing to relocate. And because a transfer is usually to another state or another country, the parents can't simply provide their own transportation to keep their child in the same school.

Integrating new students into the school occurs in three "overlapping" phases, experts say.

- The first is broad and involves procedures used with all new students, such as a tour and an orientation.
- More personalized assistance—such as invitations to join school clubs or activities and ongoing support from a peer or school staff member—might be necessary for students who continue to struggle.
- Finally, a more intense level of service may be required for students who have ongoing problems adjusting. They might be showing a lack of interest in schoolwork, have negative attitudes toward school, and resistance to getting involved in activities.

But you can create an environment in which students in military families feel welcome and supported as long as they attend your school, improving the chances that they will stay on course academically and gain skills that can help them weather the next transition in their lives.

Be aware, however, that helping military students adjust to their new surroundings is a process that can last much longer than it takes for them to learn their way around the building or remember their class schedule.

MAJOR CHALLENGES FOR MILITARY STUDENTS IN SCHOOL

It's important to understand the major areas in which complications can arise during a school move for a military child. Keep in mind, however, that the more resources your school or district provides to help military families and students with these matters, the less likely these issues will lead to problems in the classroom.

Military "Layoffs"

Another transition that some military students may encounter is becoming a nonmilitary child. Cuts to the Department of Defense's budget and the withdrawal from Iraq are leading to a reduction in troop levels, meaning that some servicemen and women who intended to stay in the military until retirement are instead looking for new careers. Educators should be aware that this could be another life-altering event for a family, and one that could result in another school transfer for a child.

Inconsistent Academic Standards: When a military student arrives in your school, it's likely that they have not learned some of the material that you have already covered this year. But it's also just as likely that they have already mastered a skill or topic that students in your school have not yet covered.

This is because there is wide variation across states in what students are expected to know and when they are expected to know it. This mismatch between schools becomes even more critical as children enter high school and begin accumulating credits for graduation. If courses or exams taken in one state are not accepted in another, students may not meet the requirements for graduation—even though they were on track in their previous school.

Extracurricular Activities: Students who participate in sports or other extracurricular activities, such as drama, chorus, or academic teams, often lose out on these activities when they relocate because they have missed tryouts or auditions, or because they do not meet eligibility criteria in their new school—even though these teams or activities are powerful vehicles for them to feel involved and make friendships in their new schools. Your involvement as a school principal may make the difference between a student being automatically excluded because he or she is deemed not eligible, and a thoughtful, inclusive approach that sends the message that military students are welcomed and appreciated in your school.

Special Education: Relocation can create a variety of challenges for a student with special needs. A student who had an individualized education program (IEP) or a 504 plan in his or her previous school may not automatically receive the same services in the new school. On the other hand, it's also possible that a child was labeled as a special education student in the last school because of problems related to having a parent in the military, and is considered a special education student in the new school for no good reason. Military family members with special needs are enrolled in the Exceptional Family Member Program, which is intended to make sure the individual's medical, emotional, and behavioral needs are met when a military member on active duty is transferred. Special education services vary, however, across civilian school districts. See our expanded section on Special Education in Chapter 3.

Parental Involvement: Just because parents are in the military does not mean they can't be involved in their child's education. In fact, surveys show that military parents are often very involved in school activities and support their children's education at home. Schools may need to recognize, however, that during times of deployment, the parent remaining at home may not be able to be as involved, or may need some flexibility regarding parent-teacher conferences, school events, or even homework. See the sidebar on the

Six Types of Parent Involvement from the National Network of Partnership Schools at Johns Hopkins University.

There are many ways in which you can promote the involvement of military parents. Some principals encourage active participation among military parents simply because they create a welcoming environment. Others allow flexible meeting schedules or use Internet tools such as Skype with parents who are deployed.

Social Adjustment: A child who moves frequently may feel that he or she doesn't want to go to the trouble of making new friends again. Military students report that wondering where they will fit in and who they will eat lunch with can create tremendous stress.

STRATEGIES FOR SCHOOLS

Here are some suggestions on how school leaders can make schools more responsive to the needs of military students. In developing and implementing

---

Six Types of Parent Involvement

According to the National Network of Partnership Schools at Johns Hopkins University, there are six different forms of parent involvement. Each one of these should be viewed with military families in mind.

Parenting: Assisting families with parenting skills and setting home conditions to support children as students. Also, assisting schools to better understand families—in this case, military families.

Communicating: Conducting effective communications from school to home and from home to school about programs and student progress (e.g., Skype).

Volunteering: Organizing volunteers and audiences to support the school and students. Providing volunteer opportunities in various locations and at various times.

Learning at Home: Involving families with their children on homework and other curriculum-related activities and decisions.

Decisionmaking: Involving families as participants in school decisions and developing parent leaders and representatives.

Collaborating with the Community: Coordinating resources and services from the community for families, students, and the school and providing services to the community.

The Welcome Packet

The Virginia Beach City Public Schools serve roughly 72,000 students—20% of which are from military families. To make these families feel more connected to their schools and to point them to local resources, the district created a Welcome Packet, which includes a letter from the superintendent and vital information regarding registration, school locations, and curriculum.

The district intends to make sure all school counselors use the packet as a reference when they welcome new families. The packet is considered a Promising Partnership Practice by the National Network of Partnership Schools at Johns Hopkins University.

some of the ideas we discuss below, consider engaging parent volunteers or older students needing service-learning credit.

The extent to which schools might need to use these strategies, however, depends on the answers to a few questions:

- Is your school located near a military base?
- How many students in your school are from military families?
- How many military students are significantly behind in meeting academic standards or exhibiting behavior problems that might be related to frequent school transitions?
- How much flexibility over funding or staff positions are you allowed in order to direct resources to the needs of military students?
- To what extent does your district already have policies and resources in place to respond to the special circumstances and needs of military students?

If your school doesn't have a lot of military students, it might not make sense to create schoolwide military-focused programs. Consider borrowing ideas from other schools with a lot of military children or working with your district colleagues to make sure the military students in your school have the support they need to be successful.

We organize these strategies into three categories: When Military Students Arrive, While They Are in Your School, and When They Leave. But some ideas will easily overlap into all three phases.

When Military Students Arrive

Quick Assessment: When new students arrive, have a quick assessment prepared for the student's grade level to determine how this child's skills and knowledge compare to the standards in your district or state. Have the assessment conducted in a comfortable, non-intimidating way within the child's first 2 days in the school to lessen the guesswork over the child's strengths and weaknesses. Provide teachers or other school staff with assessment tools and time during school hours to conduct initial assessments. If student records have already arrived, this may not be necessary.

Language Assessments: If the child is an English learner, have a plan in place for quickly assessing the child's English language skills.

Student Records: A student's official records don't always transfer in a timely way. Schools should be prepared to call the sending school to expedite the process. If your school is allowed flexibility over staff positions, someone could be assigned to handling issues related to record transfers. This person could also be the one in charge of orientation activities or other efforts to make sure students are integrating into their new school. Note that records may contain important information on the student's need for additional support and services, such as psychological help. This information may be of special importance for planning support services in your school for this individual student.

School Rules: Establish high expectations for behavior in your school, but make sure the rules, and any consequences that come with breaking the rules, are clearly communicated to new students. Be cognizant that what was permitted in the child's previous school might not be allowed in yours, so be understanding or provide more reminders during the first few weeks to allow students to adapt to your policies.

Creating a Welcome Team or Committee: One suggestion offered by researchers at the University of California, Los Angeles (Center for Mental

Administrator Spotlight:
Bill Billingsley, former principal of San Onofre School,
San Clemente, California

San Onofre is a K–8 school in the Fallbrook Union Elementary School District. The school is located on Marine Corps Base Camp Pendleton and serves a diverse population of military students.

Photo by Vickie Nelson

Making military parents feel welcome on the school site was important to Bill Billingsley when he served as principal.

"My goal is to try to keep the parents and the community as involved in our school community as I possibly can," says Billingsley, who is now director of state and federal programs for the district. "One of the most important things for military students is consistency. So no matter what is going on at home, no matter where you are in the deployment cycle, school is your bedrock. That is your consistent, safe place."

One of the simple events that the school holds to show appreciation for military parents—and to give deploying parents as much time as possible with their children—is a Valentine's Day lunch. Parents are welcome to come to the school during the lunch break and eat with their children.

For example, students Wyatt and Garett Oldham, pictured below, were able to share lunch with their dad Gunnery Sergeant Steve Oldham shortly before he was deployed.

Photo by Andrea Dawson

"The military impacts everything that goes on here at the school," Billingsley says. "It's something we embrace and celebrate in many different ways."

Health in Schools at UCLA, 2007), is to create a Welcoming Steering Committee that can work to establish procedures for activities such as greeting new students, introducing them to key adults in the school, showing them around the building, and providing them with information on resources within the community. This committee can include an administrator, a counselor, a Title I coordinator, a school psychologist or social worker, one or two teachers, a clerical staff person, and even one or two parents. The steering committee or another similar task force can address ways to monitor how military students or other highly mobile students are faring in school. If you create such a committee, consider inviting a military student or another student who has changed schools to offer their insight when the information being discussed is not confidential.

Having "Buddy" or "Ambassador" Programs: Pinpoint the students in your school that are the most likely to be friendly to a new student during the first few days, and ask them to assist the new students in finding their way around the school, learning the routines, and meeting other students. The "buddies" can give the new student a tour, introduce them to other students, and generally serve as a resource for the first few days. It can be especially helpful if these students have changed schools because of a family move in the past. Having buddies who are from military families themselves is even better. Consider assigning a staff member (perhaps someone who has military experience) to coordinate and support this effort. If possible, connect incoming students with a peer by phone or e-mail even before they arrive so they will have someone expecting them on their first day. Meet with these students periodically to gather input on complaints or problems new students have. Encourage teachers to have buddy programs in their classrooms.

Giving New Students a Map: Teens interviewed in focus groups for the Johns Hopkins University study noted that when they arrived at new schools, they would be given their classroom numbers, but no map to use as a guide.

The Military Impacted Schools Association provides workshops for educators on transition, deployment, and other issues affecting military families. Topics covered include:

- Developing Resilient Students
- Social Emotional Intelligence
- Making the Connection Before They Arrive
- Demographics of the Military

For more information, visit
http://militaryimpactedschoolsassociation.org/2/home

Supplies: Parents may not have time to purchase school supplies in the midst of a move, and your teachers probably require different materials and supplies than those at the student's last school. Even if they brought their old supplies, they might still be packed up in a box. Have starter kits with paper, pens and pencils, erasers, folders, notebooks—even a backpack—so there are no delays for students in doing their assignments. If possible, make sure teachers have extra copies of workbooks or textbooks so the student won't have to share with someone.

Meeting with New Families: Hold orientation sessions for new families so they can meet school leaders and ask questions about curriculum, school policies, or extracurricular activities. If your school has a highly transient population, such sessions could be scheduled on a monthly basis. Simply giving families handouts or a parent manual won't answer all of their questions and won't give them a chance to meet you. This approach can make the parents—and students—feel more comfortable contacting school administrators if concerns or problems come up later.

Creating a Welcome Center or Transition Room: This center, whether staffed by volunteers or a paid employee, can serve multiple purposes. Have brochures or other materials on-hand about school and community

Parent Christa Carlson, right, visits the transition center with her daughters at Akers Elementary at the Naval Air Station in Lemoore, California

Photo by Marcy Lawson

resources for both incoming students and parents. These can include special activities or programs designed for new students, such as buddy programs or tutoring, as well as child care, preschool, after-school activities, sports and camps, and employment information for parents. Recognize that when a military family moves, one of the top concerns on the parents' list might be finding employment for a spouse. You can also prepare a brief incoming survey for families to better understand their needs, such as whether one parent is deployed or is about to be deployed, if there are any subjects the student might be struggling in, or what activities the student was involved in at their last school. Finally, depending on the space you have available for this room and the hours it can be supervised, it can also serve as a retreat for new students to gather at lunch or study periods if they are still having trouble blending into the school. You could even dedicate an hour a week for a playgroup for younger siblings. While the room might be created with military families in mind, it can be useful for welcoming any new family that arrives during the school year. Read more about what the Hawaii Department of Education and the Navy school liaisons are doing at the end of this chapter.

While They Are in Your School

Troops to Teachers: One way to create connections between military families and your school's staff might be to hire a former member of the military as a member of your faculty. Troops to Teachers is a nationwide program operated by the Defense Activity for Non-Traditional Education Support (DANTES), a division within the Department of Defense. The program assists former members of the military in making the transition into a second career as a teacher, focusing specifically where there are needs for highly qualified teachers in high-needs schools. Most large states have their own Troops to Teachers offices, while some smaller states share an office. For more information, visit http://www.proudtoserveagain.com/.

Meeting Your SLO: School liaison officers work for the four branches of the military to help students in military families be academically successful. They also work with local civilian school districts to address any education-related problems or barriers that might keep students from having a positive experience. In the Marines, they are called school liaisons and for the Air Force, they are called "point-of-contact" advocates. These officers are often based on military installations, but in some cases, their offices are actually housed as part of the local school district to facilitate communication and cooperation with school officials and staff. Consider inviting them to speak to military parents at your school or to attend school events so families will recognize that they are available to help.

Forming Relationships with the Command: Make the military base your partner. Work with school liaison officers to find events or initiatives that the schools and the base can work on together. In some military communities, service members from the base offer to set up or take down equipment for events, loan materials, run field days, provide demonstrations, or provide other services that can foster a positive relationship between the base and the school. "When you have command and principals working together, you have a powerful knowledge of the needs in your school," says Pamela Hosmer, a program manager with the San Diego Unified School District.

Tutoring: If learning gaps do exist, or if the child is performing below grade level, be aware of all opportunities that your district provides to help students catch up–both during the school day and in before- or after-school programs. If your school is a Title I school, the student may also qualify for free, private tutoring through the Supplemental Educational Services provision of No Child Left Behind.

A 2010 report from the Government Accountability Office on highly mobile students showed that some school officials report using Title I, Part A funds to pay for tutoring and after-school instruction for transient students. Others used stimulus funds under the American Recovery and Reinvestment Act to hire additional teachers for small-group instruction.

If a student is in high school, explore options for credit recovery if he or she is lacking required coursework. Identify where waivers might be granted if a similar course was taken in another state or overseas. (See our section on the Interstate Compact in Chapter 3.)

As you will see in sections below, there are additional resources designed to help military students. Military bases, school liaison officers, and other organizations provide information, tutoring, and other services to help military students maximize their academic potential. Consider taking advantages of these resources to help the school supplement its efforts on behalf of military students.

Acceleration: Instead of being behind, some of your military students may have already mastered the skills being taught at their grade level. These students may need additional opportunities for enrichment and more challenging material. Consider allowing students to go into the next grade for instruction in the areas where they are advanced. This is good preparation for taking pre-Advanced Placement (AP) courses in middle school or AP courses in high school.

Attendance: Adjusting to a new school–once again–can take an emotional toll on military students. Track repeated absences and tardiness of military and other highly mobile students during the initial weeks after the

Students in the "Pride Club" at Wolf Canyon Elementary in Chula Vista, California, worked together to create a "pride board" display honoring their family members in the military

Photo by Gena Truitt

Resources for Students

The following are examples of publications that could be used in discussions or group sessions with military students.

- *My Story: Blogs by Four Military Teens,* by Michelle D. Sherman and DeAnne M. Sherman. This booklet presents the blog entries of four fictional teenagers as they write about their relationships with their military parents.
- *Finding My Way: A Teen's Guide to Living with a Parent Who Has Experienced Trauma,* by Michelle D. Sherman and DeAnne M. Sherman. This book includes lessons, activities, and resources aimed at teens.
- *While You Are Away,* by Eileen Spinelli. This picture book is appropriate for younger children. Three children, speaking in the first person, anticipate the returns of their parents, who are away on active military duty.
- *A Boy at War,* by Harry Mazer. This novel is appropriate for students in grades 5–9. It tells the story of a 14-year-old boy whose father is an officer assigned to the USS Arizona when the attack on Pearl Harbor takes place in 1941.

student's arrival. Missing days of school can make gaps in learning even worse. Make sure students and parents are quickly made aware of your school's policies regarding missed work, but also have procedures in place for allowing students to make up work if they miss school. The chances are good that some of the rules in place at the child's previous school are different than yours. (Also see Block Leave in Chapter 4.)

School Events/Displays: Find ways to honor the history and contributions of military members either in school events–perhaps with a guest speaker–or in displays prominently placed in the school building. As with Black History Month, schools that serve the military community can integrate the history and culture of the military into student learning. Some schools hold Military Appreciation events or flag salutes, and invite members of the military to attend as a way to honor these families.

Differentiation: Having teachers who are trained to meet students' differing learning needs in the same classroom can be especially beneficial for military students or other new students who are coming into the school at different points in the curriculum. Because educators recognize that all schools have grown more diverse, differentiation is an approach that is gaining more attention as a way to keep students engaged and moving forward–even if they haven't changed schools.

Instruction can be adapted in four ways:

- the content being taught
- the process and activities used to teach the content
- the product, that is the way the student demonstrates what he or she has learned
- the environment in which students learn

Looping: Research has demonstrated the academic and social benefits of keeping students with the same teacher for more than one year. Teachers

---

Honoring Veterans

The following notice was included in the parent newsletter at Olympic View Elementary School in Chula Vista, California:

"In commemoration of Veteran's Day, there will be a Wall of Heroes in the auditorium this week and next. Students who have a parent, sibling, or any other family member who has served in the military are welcome to bring a picture for our wall. Students are encouraged to write a few sentences about why they are proud of their family member."

become keenly aware of a student's learning style and stronger bonds between teachers and students can contribute to stronger academic gains. For military students—who experience multiple transitions—this type of consistency in their new school might be especially positive.

Professional Development: Provide teachers and other staff with opportunities to learn more about the unique circumstances of students who grow up in military families. Organizations such as the Military Child Education Coalition, the Military-Impacted Schools Association, and Johns Hopkins University provide training opportunities that also count as staff development credit. Perhaps find a teacher or other staff member at your school that has either had military experience or grew up in the military to help organize such training.

Having More Than One Parent-Teacher Conference: Most schools hold at least one parent-teacher conference in the fall, but not all schools hold a second one in the spring to discuss where the child is at the end of the year as they prepare for the transition to the next grade. Having at least two of these meetings is especially important for military students who are not only moving up a grade, but could be off to another school in the fall. At the middle and high school level, some schools include students in these sessions so they can talk about their own strengths and weaknesses. These meetings will help parents be better informed as they make decisions about their children's education, especially if they face another move and need to look for a new school.

Common Planning: Many schools now organize master schedules in order to allow teachers to have weekly—or more frequent—common planning periods. These sessions can be used to examine data trends, discuss curriculum and instruction issues, and communicate about the needs of individual students. Encourage teachers to consider the needs of military students during these sessions—both for coming up with teaching ideas that incorporate military history or heroes into lessons as well as determining whether there are any recurring learning issues affecting these students.

Celebrating Military-Related Events: If your school has never done anything to recognize military families and children, the Month of the Military Child or Military Family Month are great places to start. Held throughout April, the Month of the Military Child is sponsored by the Department of Defense and is used to show appreciation for the role that children play in the military community. Events often include picnics, parades, or spring festivals, but can also be as simple as having students make cards for each other or posters to hang in the school hallways. Held in November, Military Family Month is another opportunity to honor these members of your school community. Families that previously felt uncomfortable identifying themselves as military-connected may see this as an opportunity to feel proud of their service. Information on Month of the Military Child is available at http://www.nctsnet.org/resources/public-awareness/month-military-child; and for Military Family Month at http://www.whitehouse.gov/the-press-office/2011/11/01/presidential-proclamation-military-family-month-2011

Applying for Grants: The demographics of your student population often determine whether your school will qualify for particular grants. There are a variety of grants available to schools with good ideas for using the funds to support learning and to give students valuable experiences. Stacy Jones, the principal of Miller Elementary, which is located in a military family housing community in the San Diego Unified School District, is always on the lookout for grant opportunities to support her school's efforts to provide military students and families with a welcoming environment that meets their needs. When her school recently received funds for a library makeover from the Target Corporation, she used some of it to build a meeting room in the center of the library to be used as a gathering place for parents and school liaison officers. And a Healthy Start grant from the California Department of Education is being used to form a support group for parents of students with special needs. "We are always looking at what's out there and how we can get the most bang for our buck," she says.

Forming Partnerships with Community-Based Agencies: Even if your school is located near a base—where services are available for military families—parents often prefer not to go on base for programs or face

---

Finding Grants to Support Military Children

Here are a few key places to search for grant funds related to military children.

Military K–12 Partners is a DoDEA partnership program for public school districts that is intended to support research-based efforts that increase student achievement among military students and ease the challenges they face due to their parents' service in the military. http://www.militaryk12partners.dodea.edu/grants.cfm

Our Military Kids provides grants to children of National Guard and the Reserves, as well as to children of wounded warriors from all branches. The funds can be used for participation in sports, fine arts, camps, or tutoring programs while a parent is deployed or recovering from an injury. http://www.ourmilitarykids.org/

transportation obstacles to getting members of the family there during a busy school week. Explore the possibilities of health, counseling, or other providers offering services on your school site. The Coalition for Community Schools in Washington provides a variety of resources and support to schools interested in serving as a hub of services for families and communities. Visit their website at www.communityschools.org. You may have local community partners who are interested in offering some of their services for parents and children on your school site. Also, see our profile of the Escondido Union School District at the end of the Chapter 4, "Deployment."

Finishing the School Year: As said, schools have no influence over where and when the military decides to move its service members, so a student may at times need to transfer during the school year. Parents remaining at home also sometimes move to be closer to family members for additional support during a deployment. Explore with the family all options for keeping the student in the same school for the rest of the academic year.

Using Your Website: If military students are a significant population in your school or district, use your school or district website to reflect this aspect of your school community, just as you would with the racial and ethnic makeup of the families you serve. Some military-connected school districts, for example, provide links on their websites to organizations that offer resources and programs for military families. Here is an example from the Oceanside Unified School District in California: http://www.oside.k12.ca.us/cms/page_view?d=x&piid=&vpid=1281763223429

BRAC–Will It Affect Your School?

The Department of Defense is in the midst of several initiatives that involve moving large numbers of military members to several bases across the country. One of these is Base Realignment and Closure (BRAC) and another is Grow the Force.

These changes in training activities and operations will impact school districts surrounding military bases. The states to be affected are Alabama, Colorado, Florida, Georgia, Hawaii, Kansas, Kentucky, Louisiana, Maryland, Missouri, New Mexico, New York, North Carolina, Ohio, Oklahoma, Texas, Virginia, and Washington.

The National Association of Federally Impacted Schools provides an informative brochure on BRAC and its effects on the Impact Aid program. Find it in the Publications section on their website at http://www.nafisdc.org/

Morning Meetings: More common in elementary grades than at the middle and high school level, morning meetings can set the tone for the day, allow students to share news or comments with their peers, and prepare classes for the academic work of the day ahead. These time slots could be used to highlight important events for military students, such as the return of a deployed parent or if a military-related trajedy has occurred. More information on organizing and using morning meetings is available at http://responsiveclassroom.org/.

Advisory Programs: In middle and high schools, advisory programs can give students a forum for discussing a variety of issues, including friendships, dating, bullying, cultural and community issues, as well as college and career-readiness. An advisor can also serve as another adult to monitor how students are integrating into the school and can provide them with a more personalized school experience. Some schools have designed their advisory programs as clubs focused around particular themes, further allowing students to meet students with similar interests.

Monitoring Behavior: Are military students frequently being referred to your leadership team for behavior issues or breaking school rules? Are there indications that groups of military students are being picked on by other groups in your school? Examine your data and use other means such as interviews and focus groups to determine the discipline issues most likely to be affecting military students or other highly mobile students.

Learning from the Child: A military child has probably lived somewhere else that you and other students in your school have not–possibly even overseas. If you have a student advisory committee, invite a military student to be part of it. They may be able to bring ideas from past schools they have attended that you haven't considered. Or, encourage military students to be involved in student government or take on other leadership responsibilities.

Extracurricular Activities: Have policies in place that give military students or other highly mobile students an opportunity to be involved in sports or other extracurricular activities, even after tryouts or other sign-up periods have ended. Accept letters of recommendation or videos of performances as evidence of a student's abilities. (See our section on the Interstate Compact in Chapter 3.) Special classes, sports, or other activities can assist students in developing friendships and can help to ease the stress related to relocating or a parent's deployment. A coach or an instructor can also play the important role of serving as another adult for military children to talk to and monitor how children are adjusting.

2. Mobility

Yearbooks, T-Shirts, Etc.: Schools often require families to purchase items such as yearbooks or school "spirit wear" during the early weeks of the school year. If you have a highly transient school, purchase extras so new students can still have a memento if they wish. Even if they weren't at the school when yearbook pictures were taken, they can still have an important memorable item for their friends to sign. If they leave the school before yearbooks come out, make arrangements to send them one after their friends or teachers have had a chance to sign it. Highland Ranch Elementary School in the Poway Unified School District in Southern California goes even further by dedicating a special page within its yearbook to honor students' parents who are serving in the military.

When They Leave

Recognizing the Patterns: Permanent Change of Station orders for military members often follow predictable patterns. For military children, this can mean that when their family transfers from one installation to another, they are likely to end up near other students they already know from their past community. In the Navy, for example, military personnel often move from the Sasebo base in Japan to Naval Air Station Sigonella in Sicily and then to an assignment in San Diego, California. Becoming familiar with these patterns and collaborating with other principals to find ways for families to reconnect with each other—even if they're not in the same school—tells them that you want their transition to go as smoothly as possible.

Partnering with Parents

Military parents in your school can be an excellent resource for organizing special events or connecting with military organizations. When Pilar Byham, principal of Temecula Elementary School in Temecula, California, wanted to hold a Military Appreciation Day, she involved Marine wife Andrea Sullivan, who was helpful in scheduling a visit by the Marine Corps Color Guard.

Photo by Eric Lindberg

District Spotlight: San Diego Unified School District

Requests for services or information for military families used to get lost in the system at the San Diego Unified School District. That's because no one at the central office was directly responsible for handling those calls and coordinating resources for San Diego's large military community, explains Pamela Hosmer, a program manager with the district who focuses on children and youth in transition.

When the district received a grant from the DoDEA, Hosmer was put in charge of those requests, and this became the district's first step toward creating a structure to support military students and a network of military and community agencies with services to provide.

Hosmer learned that bringing services into schools—rather than expecting parents to seek help at community agencies—was sometimes a more efficient and comfortable method for military families.

"Even though a school might be right next to a base doesn't mean the parents will go to the base for services," Hosmer says.

A "military collaborative" in San Diego now includes over 100 agencies and providers that work with military families and includes the school liaison officers. The collaborative meets regularly—another practice that Hosmer says is necessary to keep communication flowing.

Once this structure was created, the district was better able to assess the needs of individual schools and involve principals in determining what services or programs would meet the needs of their students.

"Once we had something to offer [principals], it created a dialogue," Hosmer says. "The principals help each other."

Several schools, for example, have created "connections rooms" which serve as welcome and resource centers for new families. See our feature on these rooms at the end of this chapter. Those schools without specific rooms have at least created a consistent process that they use to welcome new students and parents. Other schools have implemented the Student2Student (S2S) program. S2S is an initiative of the Military Child Education Coalition in which students are trained to serve as mentors to others who are transitioning in or out of schools.

Other practices include creating memory books for students who are leaving and planting friendship gardens as a way to connect students with friends who have moved.

In addition to informing principals of the organizations that offer services, the district also makes sure that parents are aware of the many agencies and programs available. The district holds "enrollment fairs" for families that arrive in the district late in the summer, after typical enrollment activities have already taken place. Organizations set up booths and provide information, making it easy for families to find out about their programs. You may want to suggest these practices to your district or perhaps initiate some of them in your own school.

The San Diego district's "enrollment fair"

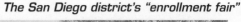

Photo by
Kimberly Shapazian

The district also tracks its military student population as part of its student information system—a tool that has significantly raised awareness among principals about the needs of these families, Hosmer says. In fact, now when principals are planning for staff for the coming school year, they ask the district for enrollment projections for military students.

"You've got to know who the kids are, where the kids are," Hosmer says, "And then make sure the principals are aware."

The SETS Project

The Secondary Education Transition Study—a joint project between the Army and the Military Child Education Coalition (MCEC)—documented the effects of school transition specifically for high school students. Released in 2001, the study showed wide variation in how schools handle the transfer and interpretation of student records. Inconsistencies in school schedules and calendars increased the chances of problematic transitions.

Solutions recommended included allowing parents to hand carry student records to make sure they arrive with the student, having virtual tours of schools or new student orientations online, and providing options for enhanced or alternate diplomas and earning graduation credit.

MCEC is currently updating the study with new research.

RESEARCH HIGHLIGHTS ON STUDENT MOBILITY

Below are some key findings on student mobility in general and on military students.

- A 1993 study by Dr. David Wood, at the time a professor of pediatrics at Cedars-Sinai Medical Center in Los Angeles, showed that children who changed schools at least six times between 1st and 12th grade were 35% more likely to fail a grade than children who didn't change schools or those who had only moved a couple of times during that period.
- The University of Chicago's David Kerbow wrote in 2003 that highly mobile students were an average of 4 months behind their less transient classmates on standardized tests by 4th grade. By the 6th grade, students who were highly mobile during elementary school lagged behind their classmates by as much as a full year.
- More recently, a study from researchers at the University of Michigan (Burkam, Lee, & Dwyer, 2009) used data from the Early Childhood Longitudinal Study–Kindergarten Cohort, a large sample of over 30,000 children, to examine the impact of mobility on children in the early grades. In the full sample, changing schools does not appear to have serious detrimental effects on children's learning. However, examining effects by certain groups showed that children of lower socioeconomic status face greater academic setbacks when they change schools duri-ng kindergarten, but those who repeat kindergarten may show learning gains when they change schools. Children who are receiving special education services typically do worse after they change schools.
- In 2010, Catherine P. Bradshaw and colleagues from Johns Hopkins University found that adolescents from military families experience significant stress related to making school transitions, from worrying about maintaining past friendships and forming new ones, to feeling lost in class because they haven't covered certain material. In focus groups, students talked about learning how to "blend in" to new social situations and seeking out other military students. School staff members interviewed commented that military students in high school appear more mature than other students their age.
- Allan M. O'Brien from the Peabody College for Teachers at Vanderbilt University examined the relationship between mobility and achievement in a New York school district adjacent to the Fort Drum Army base in 2007. About half of the district's 4,000 students are military children. The study showed that while mobility can have negative effects on military children's performance, outcomes

significantly improve when children have "rich social support networks." This can include the attitudes of parents—especially mothers—regarding the move and whether information is available about the school and community where the child is going.

- In a 2008 study, Diana H. Gruman from Western Washington University found that the most important factor in a new student's adjustment to school is the teacher(s). Those who were supportive of highly mobile students had a strong influence on their attitudes toward school and on their behavior in the classroom. The researchers recommended intensive tutoring for new students in case of academic deficits and professional development for teachers so they can better understand the challenging circumstances faced by mobile students.

RESOURCES FOCUSING ON MILITARY CHILDREN

Listed below are organizations, programs, and publications that can provide more insight into many of the issues students from military families face.

Honoring Our Heroes

Photos by Diana Pineda

Jennifer Aynesworth, principal of Vintage Hills Elementary School in Temecula, California, addresses students and parents at a Memorial Day "flag salute." The schoolwide event honors military members who have died in service to our country and recognizes current military parents who are part of the school community. Several military dads also attended the event.

Military Child Education Coalition (MCEC): This is a worldwide organization focused on ensuring quality educational opportunities for all military-connected children affected by mobility, family separation, and transition. The MCEC performs research, develops resources, conducts professional institutes and conferences, and publishes resources for all constituencies. http://www.militarychild.org/

Department of Defense Education Activity: A field activity of the Office of the Secretary of Defense, DoDEA operates schools for the children of military members stationed at bases in both the United States and overseas. This website provides information on current initiatives within the schools, an overview of curriculum, a data center, and links to all 194 schools. http://www.dodea.edu/home/about.cfm

Building Resilient Kids: This online Internet course from Johns Hopkins University is designed to help school administrators, teachers, and faculty to be more aware of the special needs of children who come from military families. http://www.jhsph.edu/mci/training_course/

School Connectedness: Improving Students' Lives: As part of the Military Child Initiative at the Johns Hopkins University Bloomberg School of Public Health, three publications discuss practices that can help students feel more connected to their schools. There is a monograph, an executive summary, and a tip sheet for teachers. http://www.jhsph.edu/mci/resources/School_Connectedness

Tackling Tough Topics: An Educator's Guide to Working with Military Kids: This booklet was developed by the Washington State Office of the Superintendent of Public Instruction. https://www.operationmilitarykids.org/resources/ToughTopics%20BookletFINAL.pdf

Military Family Research Institute: Located at Purdue University, the MFRI is a research and outreach organization focusing on quality of life issues for military families. http://www.cfs.purdue.edu/mfri/public/default.aspx

Military Students on the Move: A Toolkit for School Leaders: This manual is written for school leaders, but also provides valuable information for teachers on how to help their military-impacted students cope with relocation and make the transition process easier for students and their families. http://hanscomservices.com/graphics/School%20Liaison/PDFs/A-Toolkit-for-School-Leaders_2012.pdf

2. Mobility

Leveling the Playing Field for Military Connected Students: This PowerPoint presentation provides a brief overview of the issues military children face and ways schools can respond. http://www.militaryk12partners. dodea.edu/docs/reference_leveling.pdf

Operation Military Kids: This handout, focusing on students whose parents are in the National Guard and Reserves, provides a quick overview to help educators become sensitive to the unique culture of military children and their families. http://www.extension.umn.edu/FamilyRelations/components/OMK_LC_handout.pdf

Handbook for Garrison Commanders and Reference for School Superintendents: An MCEC publication, this handbook focuses specifically on the Army and is a useful primer for school leaders needing to understand more about how the military functions and about why a "disconnect" between civilian schools and military families exists. Search for it in MCEC's online Library at http://www.militarychild.org/library

Special Education Professional Development: As part of its Partnership Program, DoDEA has created training modules for educators in civilian schools focusing on issues such as autism, conducting special education assessments, and Response to Intervention. http://www.militaryk12partners. dodea.edu/resources.cfm?colId=sped

Student Mobility: This is a thoughtful collection of research highlights and suggested recommendations from the Leon County Schools in Florida. http://www.tandl.leon.k12.fl.us/programme/mobility.html

Students at the Center: This guide from DoDEA's Military K–12 Partners website speaks to the various groups involved in helping military students be successful: parents, civilian school officials, and military leaders. The section for educators includes information on the military branches, the Impact Aid program, and basic military terms. http://www.militaryk12partners. dodea.edu/studentsAtTheCenter/index.html

BRATS: Our Journey Home: This documentary, featuring Kris Kristofferson and Norman Schwarzkopf, provides a glimpse into the experiences of children who have grown up in military households. Brats Without Borders, the nonprofit organization that produced the film, has an outreach effort, Operation Military Brat, which offers workshops to educators and other groups to raise awareness about what it's like to grow up as a military child. http://www.bratsourjourneyhome.com/index.htm

Building Capacity in Military-Connected Schools: A part of the Do-DEA project at USC that led to the creation of this guidebook, this website provides information on programs for military students, ongoing research, videos, and newsletters featuring practices that public schools can implement to help military children and families feel more welcome and supported. http://buildingcapacity.usc.edu/

Promising Practice Spotlight:
Central Union School District's Transition Specialist

Two of the four schools in the Central Union School District, near Fresno, California, are located on the base of the Naval Air Station in Lemoore. Almost 100% of the students served by Akers Elementary and Neutra Elementary are from military families.

With a grant from DoDEA, the district has established a Transition Specialist position to focus on welcoming new students, monitoring their adjustment into their new school, and responding to any ongoing issues the students are having either academically, socially, or emotionally.

The position is held by Anne Gonzales, a vice-principal at Akers who also has a background as a school social worker.

"Students are coming from everywhere and they come from many, many different special circumstances and stressors," she says. "We do see the need for addressing transition."

Transition Specialist Anne Gonzales, top right, meets with Christa Carlson and her daughters Riley, bottom left, and Trinity. The girls entered Akers Elementary on the Naval Air base during the school year.

Photo by Mary Lawson

Gonzales meets with every new student and their parents—sometimes even on the day they come in to register. She has to assure them that when they are called to her office that it is not because they are in trouble. She will review transcripts—especially those of middle grade students—to see if there are any gaps in their schooling and talk to the students about whether they understand what is being taught in their new classes and whether they are making friends.

While most of the 1,300 students at the two schools live in housing on the base, some live in surrounding neighborhoods, which can also affect their peer group and what they are doing after school.

New students are part of her "caseload" for three months, but if a student demonstrates a need for ongoing support, she remains involved.

On a typical day, Gonzales meets with 8–10 students, and might also talk with the same number of parents. She also participates in IEP meetings and works with teachers to discuss ways to differentiate instruction for students.

Because her district only serves students through 8th grade, she hasn't spent a lot of time focusing on students' transition into high school. But Akers, a pre-K–8 school, does offer an elective class called "Strategies for Academic Success." It is similar to the AVID (Advancement via Individual Determination) program in that it focuses on college and career readiness.

Gonzales' experience demonstrates that even on a base, with all of the family support services the military offers, there is still a role for public schools to play in helping students and their families make successful transitions into their new schools.

She added that other schools serving military students can also implement many of the practices that she is using. "The strategies and the things that I do can be replicated in any setting," she says. "You just have to start with an awareness."

Making Connections

According to *Connections: Navy School Based Programming Guidebook*, the following components should be part of a comprehensive school-based support program for military families:

School Entry: This includes providing a welcome kit, assessing academic needs, and surveying students about their interests.

Youth Sponsorship: New students are assigned a "sponsor" or mentor, which can be another student, to help them become acclimated and during times of need, such as during a parent's deployment.

Deployment Support: This can include a needs survey, counseling
services, support groups, peer lunch groups, and helping students
communicate with the deployed parent about school-related activities.

Family Component: Parent orientation, volunteer opportunities, monthly
activities, and workshops would be in this category.

Ongoing Monitoring: Depending on the student's and family's needs,
monitoring can last as long as a year.

Exit Process: Gather information on the next school and community,
compile the records, contact the next school, and conduct an exit
assessment.

2. Mobility

Promising Practice Spotlight: Hawaii's Parent Community Network Coordinators, San Diego's Connections Rooms, and the "Family Readiness Express"

With all branches of the armed services represented in Hawaii, the state
has some of the most heavily military-impacted public schools in the
country.

Roughly 8% of the state's public school enrollment—15,000
students—come from military families. Addressing their unique
educational needs is what led to the development of a military liaison
position at the Hawaii Department of Education in 2004 and the creation
of the Parent Community Network Coordinator (PCNC) program at dozens
of schools throughout the state.

Of the 57 schools with the highest numbers of military students,
50 have PCNCs. Most also have a separate staff person in the role of a
transition coordinator.

Local school decisionmaking is a key feature of Hawaii's schools, but
generally, PCNCs are in place to welcome new families, orient them to
the school, and answer any questions they might have about rules, school
activities, and community resources.

"It's really important for these parents when they come in to feel
some connectivity," says Cherise Imai, the state education department's
military liaison, describing these staff members as "the heartbeat of the
school."

Scaling Up

Hawaii's leadership in improving school climate for military students
has also inspired a broader initiative by Navy School Liaison Officers to
implement best practices for helping military families transition into new

schools. This effort is featured in the new *Connections: Navy School Based Programming Guidebook,* available at https://acrobat.com/app.html#d=UvP*UK3qJ39DUohoULionw.

The Hawaii model is being successfully implemented at schools in the San Diego area.

At Perry Elementary School, located in the Bayview Hills military housing community in San Diego, parent volunteer and Navy wife Rachel Wohnhaas runs the school's Fox's Den—a "connections" room used to help new families become familiar with the school. Just off the playground, the spacious room has plenty of seating, games and puzzles for small children, and a computer station where students can use Skype to communicate with a deployed parent. Wohnhaas, or another volunteer, gives new students a brief questionnaire to find out what they like to do and even whether they have any allergies. She also gives the families a tour and makes sure the new students have a buddy to show them around. She finds out, however, that these initial acquaintances don't usually turn into strong friendships. Instead they serve more as a bridge to help the new student meet others.

Rachel Wohnhaas welcomes new families to Perry Elementary's "Fox's Den"

Photo by
Linda Jacobson

"If they gel, they gel. If they don't, they don't," Wohnhaas says. "You don't force the issue."

At Dewey Elementary, which backs up to a military housing complex, School Liaison Officer Robin Williamson has been given less room to work with, but has still made the school's "connections corner" a welcoming spot with a sofa, patriotic décor, and a large teddy bear that is likely to attract young children.

New families receive a survey to determine deployment status or whether the student might need tutoring. Williamson also makes sure they find out about local activities and ways to get involved. Doing research on schools before she moved and volunteering in her three children's schools, she says, is how she has weathered repeated relocations. She was surprised to realize recently that her daughter, a sophomore in high school, has actually attended nine schools—the number often cited in studies about military children.

Robin Williamson makes Dewey's new "connections corner" a welcoming place

Photo by
Linda Jacobson

Shannon Milder, a regional School Liaison Officer for Commander Navy Region Southwest, finds that the key to a successful connections room is support from the school's principal and strong parent involvement.

A Place to "Hang Out"

As with Wohnhaas and Williamson, many PCNCs in Hawaii schools are military spouses, so they can relate to what the new families are experiencing. Some of the coordinators even work as volunteers; it depends on the school and how they decide to fund the program.

Transition coordinators at the schools, who work in tandem with the PCNCs, tend to handle issues related to placement and academic records.

"Sometimes, [the students] come in with nothing," Imai says.

At the high school level, the PCNCs place an increased focus on making sure students are blending socially into the school. The centers where these coordinators work also serve as a "hang-out room," especially during lunch—a time in the day that for many transient students can create stress.

Imai says some students come to the center to eat their lunch because they haven't quite bonded with other students yet, or just because they prefer a quiet place.

With so many solid programs for incoming students, Imai said many PCNCs are now recognizing the need to expand their services for students that are preparing to leave. In Hawaiian tradition, some schools now present students with a farewell lei, just as they would when they are welcoming someone for the first time.

For more information on Hawaii's efforts, visit http://militaryfamily. k12.hi.us/. For San Diego area efforts visit http://buildingcapacity.usc. edu/

Mobile Support

In addition to the connections rooms in military-impacted schools in San Diego, families in the region have an added resource operated by the Navy's Fleet and Family Support division. The Family Readiness Express—a luxury RV equipped with resources for military families—travels to military housing communities, usually staying for a month at a time, to provide support, information, and answers to family members' questions.

Currently the only unit of its kind in the country, the RV was put into service in 2010.

"The Navy bought it, but we're there for everyone—for all branches," said Dana Ross, the former program operations manager.

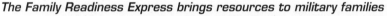

The Family Readiness Express brings resources to military families

Photo by
Linda Jacobson

One area of the vehicle is stocked with books for children, another provides resources related to employment, and another area focuses on deployment support.

By partnering with community organizations, this "traveling billboard," as Tammie Pontsler, the education services coordinator, called it, can provide a variety of workshops, such as parenting or financial seminars, as well as one-on-one advice. Other services and activities have included free bread distribution, coloring contests for children, and participation in family-oriented events.

The Family Readiness Express visits
Jefferson Middle School in Oceanside, California

Photo by
Diana Pineda

In the fall of 2011, the staff also brought the eye-catching mobile support unit to schools surrounding Camp Pendleton to provide teachers and families with an additional way to access the resources available. Having the "Express" on campus was a great way to "put a face" on the programs that are available to military families, said Justin Kern, assistant principal at Jefferson Middle School in Oceanside. "There are a lot of resources out there, but the thing is connecting them," he said, adding that the visit was a wonderful opportunity for all the students—not just those with a parent in the military. "A lot of these kids have issues that go beyond the four walls of the classroom."

2. Mobility

CHAPTER 3

Policy Issues

This chapter focuses on the role of education policy in supporting military students. As an administrator, it is important for you to know how your state and district stands on many of these issues. Some of these refer to existing policies that can be adapted to respond to the needs of military students. Other policies have been developed specifically for military students, but are not used to their full potential.

The following topics are covered:

- Lessons from Federal Programs for Highly Mobile Students
- Common Core Standards
- Common Education Data Standards
- The Interstate Compact on Educational Opportunity for Military Children
- Supporting Military Students with Special Needs
- Lessons from DoDEA Schools
- Impact Aid

LESSONS FROM FEDERAL PROGRAMS FOR HIGHLY MOBILE STUDENTS

The education community can learn from practices and policies designed to meet the needs of other students facing frequent transitions. For example, the McKinney-Vento Homeless Education Assistance Act requires schools to have a liaison to ensure that homeless students are enrolled in school–even if all required documents are not available–and that homeless students and their families receive appropriate services. Similarly, schools with large proportions of military children can designate a staff member or volunteer as a liaison–someone who becomes familiar with common pressing issues and has the knowledge or the connections with other agencies to resolve problems. This person can be the primary contact for the school liaison officers who work for the branches of the military.

Randy Garcia, the director of pupil services for the Escondido Union School District, looks to McKinney-Vento as a model for serving military families by:

- providing a liaison to better connect them with the school and help them receive tutoring, counseling, medical care, housing, and other resources
- allowing students to remain in their school even if their parent moves or is deployed to ensure a consistent and stable learning environment
- allowing families to choose their preferred school through a School of Choice process
- adopting a school board policy and administrative regulation explaining how military students will be served and supported throughout the district

As another example, the Migrant Student Records Exchange Initiative–part of the No Child Left Behind Act–created a system in which states can share educational and health information on migrant children who move between states and, as a result, have official records in more than one state. The technology facilitates school enrollment and grade placement, and makes sure students receive credit for courses taken–all of which are issues that military children also encounter. The purpose of the program is to "ensure greater continuity of educational services for migrant children by providing a mechanism for all states to exchange education-related information on migrant children who move from state to state due to their migratory lifestyle," according to the Department of Education. The system also allows states to notify each other when a migrant student is moving to a different state. Such a system would also be valuable for schools receiving large numbers of military students. An effort to create Common Education Data Standards, launched by a consortium of organizations including the Council of Chief State School Officers and the Data Quality Campaign, has similar goals–allowing educators to quickly understand a student's academic performance in order to keep the student moving forward. (See more information on Common Education Data Standards later in this chapter.)

COMMON CORE STATE STANDARDS

When military children attend one of the 194 DoDEA schools around the world–whether it's McBride Elementary on Ft. Benning in Georgia or Boeblingen Elementary in Heidelberg, Germany–they are taught the same curriculum, and are assessed using the same tests, which allows for comparisons among students.

This uniformity is in place so that military children, who often must pick up and change schools with little advance preparation, won't fall behind in school, or conversely have to repeat material that they've already mastered.

This creates a predictable situation for families who tend to have unpredictable lives.

Currently in the United States, each state sets its own standards for what students are expected to learn as they progress through school. But this system has led to wide variation across the country, and students—not just those in the military, but anyone who moves from state to state—sometimes experience redundancy in lessons or far worse, miss out on entire subjects.

The Common Core State Standards is an effort led by two national organizations—the Council of Chief State School Officers and the National Governors Association—to develop clear and consistent guidelines for what students are expected to learn and to prepare them for college and careers.

The Common Core, in effect, mirrors the approach already used by the DoDEA schools. Supporters of the Common Core, which the Obama administration is urging states to adopt, say that in addition to allowing for comparison of student performance across the country, the Core also makes it easier for educators to share best practices about instruction.

Accommodating the needs of military students—and other highly mobile populations—was actually part of the rationale behind the development of the Common Core.

In a letter of endorsement, Mary M. Keller, the president and CEO of the Military Child Education Coalition, wrote about why the initiative makes sense for military students.

> As military assignments or family circumstances resulting from a
> parent's deployment lead to school moves, parents and students need
> to be confident that these transitions will not increase turbulence in
> students' lives or endanger their opportunity to achieve. They also need
> to know that no matter where they attend school, they will have the
> chance to master those concepts and skills that ensure successful study at
> the post-secondary level and prepare them to enter the world of work.

Obviously, if all U.S. states adopt the Common Core standards, this would address many of the obstacles that military children moving between installations in the United States currently face, such as repeating or missing academic material and transferring credit for courses taken.

But that may or may not happen. At the time of publication, 45 states had adopted the Common Core.

And even if they did, the Common Core at this point only includes standards in math and English/language arts and doesn't address social studies, science, or other subjects.

Nevertheless, the Common Core standards provide some solutions for military students—and others who relocate often—that can minimize the disruption in their educational progress.

COMMON EDUCATION DATA STANDARDS

Military families are keenly aware that states and even local school districts vary tremendously on the information they require when a new student enrolls in school. But clearly military families are not the only ones who move from state to state and have to cope with record-keeping procedures that were different in their previous school.

That's why the Common Education Data Standards (CEDS) initiative was launched–to create a core set of preschool, K–12 and K–12 to postsecondary variables that could be easily compared and understood from state to state. One presentation by the initiative describes it as creating "an integrated profile of each learner that can be passed seamlessly" among institutions and between states.

Partners in the effort include the National Center for Education Statistics, several state and local education agencies, the Council of Chief State School Officers, State Higher Education Executive Officers, and other organizations that focus on education data.

One example given to emphasize the need for common data standards is Hurricane Katrina, after which thousands of students dispersed to other states and districts across the South, creating a pressing need for administrators and teachers in their new schools to quickly and accurately obtain their records and place them in classes appropriately. This scenario is nothing new for military parents and students.

The CEDS effort is voluntary and is still a work in progress. While it wasn't designed solely with military families in mind, it is a response to many of the complications they face when changing schools on short notice.

To learn more about the initiative and what you can do to move it forward, visit: http://www.commoneddatastandards.org/.

THE INTERSTATE COMPACT ON EDUCATIONAL OPPORTUNITY FOR MILITARY CHILDREN

Unlike their civilian peers, children from military families change schools almost every 3 years, the consequences of which vary depending on the age and level of the child. For example, at the kindergarten level, military children may begin the school year in one state, where the enrollment guidelines allow a student to enter kindergarten just after turning 5. But then they might transfer mid-year to a school in a state with a much earlier cut-off date for turning 5–suddenly making the child too young for kindergarten.

In the early grades, differences in state policy, while problematic, are to a degree benign. As military children progress in school, however, the

3. Policy Issues

The Interstate Compact on Educational Opportunity for Military Children is designed to facilitate or provide for:

- the timely enrollment of children [from] military families and [ensure] that they are not placed at a disadvantage due to difficulty in the transfer of education records between schools or variations in entrance/age requirements
- the student placement process through which children of military families are not disadvantaged by variations in attendance requirements, scheduling, sequencing, grading, course content, or assessment
- the qualification and eligibility for enrollment, educational programs, and participation in extracurricular academic, athletic, and social activities
- the on-time graduation of children of military families
- promulgation and enforcement of administrative rules implementing the provisions of [the] compact
- for the uniform collection and sharing of information between and among member states, schools, and military families under [the] compact
- coordination between this compact and other compacts affecting military children
- flexibility and coordination between the educational system, parents, and the student in order to achieve educational success for the student

Source: Council of State Governments, 2008

stakes associated with ill-aligned policies become higher and produce unintended consequences for children from military families. For example, to earn a high school diploma, many states require that graduating seniors complete a course in state history (e.g., California state history in California). Military children who begin their senior year in one state and transfer to a high school in a different state may not fulfill that requirement in time to earn their high school diploma—a reality that may limit their postsecondary opportunities.

Prior to April 2008, states lacked a uniform policy to address the needs of military children in transition. Issues related to enrollment, course/program placement, eligibility, and graduations were generally addressed on a case-by-case basis. While the Department of Defense had long worked with individual school districts, primarily those with high military enrollments, to reduce the difficulties associated with student transition, stakeholders and policymakers agreed that much more could and needed to be done at both the state and local level. They hoped that once enacted, an interstate compact–a contractual agreement entered into by two or more states in areas that are traditionally protected by state sovereignty (e.g., on education policy)–would supersede conflicting state laws related to the transition of military children from school to school and across state lines.

The purpose of the Interstate Compact on Educational Opportunity for Military Children is to reduce and/or eliminate "barriers to educational success" for children from military families as they transition between schools and across state lines.

The compact also provides for the creation of individual state councils and an interstate commission. According to the Council of State Governments (2008), unless otherwise specified, the Interstate Compact applies to:

- the children of active duty military personnel
- members of the uniformed services, including the four main branches as well as the Commissioned Corps of the National Oceanic and Atmospheric Administration, and Public Health Services
- veterans of the uniformed services who are "medically discharged or retired" up to "one year after medical discharge or retirement"
- children of "members of the uniformed services who" are deceased as a result of their service within the past year.

As of this writing, 39 states have endorsed the Interstate Compact. While the responsiveness of states to the compact is a positive development, implementing it at the local level has been challenging. An organizational structure, however, is emerging and continues to evolve. Despite having endorsed this legislation, some states have done so only symbolically and have not informed district superintendents and/or school personnel of the compact's policy implications. In the absence of state action, however, some districts have begun to implement their own policies to ease the transition of military children.

As an administrator in a school with military children, you may want to inquire whether your state has endorsed the Interstate Compact. It's also important to find out whether your district has developed any policies, practices, and resources designed to ease academic transitions of military children.

Broadly conceived, the goal of the Interstate Compact is to provide systemic support to military children in the areas that have historically been problematic for these families–enrollment, placement, eligibility, and graduation. Gaps in the dissemination of information and implementation, however, hinder the ability of civilian public schools to provide consistent support to military children. Moving forward, greater awareness and understanding of the compact is needed. School officials can support this process by learning more about the compact, its policy implications, and the resources that

are available. For more information on the Interstate Compact, visit www.
mic3.net.

[The above material is an excerpt from M. C. Esqueda, R. A. Astor, &
K. De Pedro (2012). A call to duty: Educational policy and school reform addressing the needs of children from military families. *Educational Researcher,
41*(2), 65–70.]

SUPPORTING MILITARY STUDENTS WITH SPECIAL NEEDS

Changing schools frequently is difficult for all military families. The experience can present even more challenges for students with special needs.

IDEA and the IEP

The Individuals with Disabilities Education Act (IDEA) mandates that
students with disabilities who qualify for specialized services be provided
with a free and appropriate education in the least restrictive environment.
Under the IDEA, a parent along with a team of educators draft a student's
individualized educational program (IEP). An IEP documents a student's
disability eligibility status, and school- and classroom-based supports, such as
testing accommodations, annual academic goals, and other specialized services (e.g., for speech and language). The IDEA requires that an IEP team,
which is comprised of a parent, teachers, a school administrator and other
credentialed or designated instructional services staff, such as an occupational therapist, draft a new IEP at least annually and make a comprehensive
evaluation every 3 years.

In addition, parents have the right to call for changes to an existing IEP
or to call a meeting to discuss drafting a new plan if they feel the services
their child is receiving need to change.

For military families, this entire process is repeated multiple times and
educators in one district may not always see the situation the same way as
those in the child's previous school. Realize as well that military children
often face increased stress and trauma that may result in poor learning and
behavior outcomes. Educators and other professionals should consider these
factors when determining whether a child requires special services.

Timely and Accurate Information

Making sure schools receive as much information as possible in a timely
manner is a key to ensuring that military students are served appropriately.
Some school districts such as the Los Angeles Unified School District utilize a
secured online system to track current and past IEPs. These tracking systems

assist schools in identifying incoming students with IEPs and monitoring the progress of current students with IEPs. However, not all school districts have an online tracking system, and often, incoming students with IEPs are not identified. More school districts—especially those serving highly mobile students—should implement such a model. In addition, numerous steps can be taken to make sure there is a smooth transition between schools. When enrolling a new student, school officials should routinely ask whether the student has any special needs or had an IEP in their previous school. Under the IDEA policy, parents can call an IEP meeting during the first 30 days of the student's attendance at the new school, but with so many issues to take care of during a move—especially if one parent is deployed—the family may not get to this important task.

When the meeting is held, a new IEP can be drafted to fit the student's needs within the school's existing programs. In addition, when families are leaving your district, you can assist them in the process by contacting the new school with information about the child's needs.

The Exceptional Family Member Program

School officials should also become familiar with the military's Exceptional Family Member Program (EFMP), in which the needs of military family members requiring special medical, developmental, emotional, or other services are considered when a serviceman or woman is transferred. Military members on active duty are required to enroll in this program, but it is independent from school special education programs and there may be limited communication between the two—especially in communities not located near a military installation.

Some installations have an EFMP liaison that assists families with enrolling in the program and making sure their family member receives the services they need. This person can work in tandem with a school district's special education directors on behalf of students with special needs. You may want to ask whether such a liaison is available to your school, so that you can work together to help students in your school who have special needs.

In addition, there are a variety of resources available to inform both educators and parents about making sure military-connected students with special needs receive the best care and education possible.

- **STOMP**, which stands for Specialized Training of Military Parents, is a nationwide parent training and information center for military families. The project aims to "empower military parents, individuals with disabilities, and service providers with knowledge, skills, and resources so that they might access services to create a collaborative environment for family and professional partnerships without regard to geographic location." One component of President Obama's "Strengthening Our Military Families" directive is to continue the implementation of the STOMP initiative. http://www.stompproject.org/

- **The MilitaryHOMEFRONT** website provides a listing of EFMP/ special needs contacts for all military installations both in the United States and overseas. http://www.militaryhomefront.dod.mil/portal/ page/mhf/MHF/MHF_DETAIL_1?section_id=20.40.500.570.0.0.0. 0.0&content_id=180334
- **"Understanding the Special Education Process as a Military Parent"** is a four-part guide available on the MilitaryOneSource.mil website. Click on Career & Education, Special Needs in Education and Advocating in the Schools. http://www.militaryonesource.mil

LESSONS FROM DoDEA SCHOOLS

With 194 schools in 14 countries, Department of Defense Education Activity schools were created to respond to the specific needs of highly mobile military children. But that doesn't mean civilian school districts with military students can't learn from some of their practices.

DoDEA schools have been recognized for having high overall achievement, regularly scoring above the national average on the National Assessment of Educational Progress. While gaps do exist in performance between Black and White students and Hispanic and White students, the gaps are smaller than in regular public schools.

But this system—roughly the size of a large urban school district—achieves these results in spite of experiencing high student turnover, an average of about 37% a year. There are also other statistics to consider:

- While the educational levels of enlisted personnel have been increasing, parents of DoDEA students are generally not highly educated or highly paid. The majority of DoDEA students have a parent who is an enlisted member of the military, not an officer.
- DoD Domestic Dependent Elementary and Secondary Schools, the domestic system, has a larger percentage of minority students than their public school counterparts. But their students still score above the national average in reading and writing.

The question for education leaders is: What do DoDEA schools do that allows military students to be successful in spite of the complicated lives that many of them lead?

In their 2003 study, "It's a Way of Life for Us: High Mobility and High Achievement in Department of Defense Schools," Vanderbilt University researchers Claire E. Smrekar and Debra E. Owens suggest that DoDEA has created a culture of high expectations for students that is complemented by treating high mobility as "'a way of life' rather than an intractable problem."

"The foundation of institutional and community stability in the DoDEA system includes several structural supports—some that represent effective levers for educational policymakers and others that signal unique features of the military community," they write.

Accessible Student Records

For schools with high student turnover, the timely transfer of student records poses as one of the greatest challenges to making sure students have a smooth transition into a new school. DoDEA schools have created a standardized process to ensure that there is as little delay as possible in students' learning.

"We put a lot of focus on trying to get a lot of information to the next school before the student arrives," says Mike Lynch, the chief of policy and legislation at DoDEA.

At the elementary level, parents carry their child's official records by hand to the next school, while the sending school keeps a copy.

At the middle and high school level, a student's transcript is electronically transferred to the receiving school—allowing for no interruption in educational services.

DoDEA schools have also worked to eliminate what Lynch calls "homegrown" forms—those locally created documents or permission slips that schools often require in order for students to be enrolled.

Lynch adds that when a student is transferring to another DoDEA school, teachers or school administrators often communicate with the receiving school if they think there is a particular educational or adjustment issue that could create problems for the child at the new school.

Communication between DoDEA and civilian schools when a child is transferring from one to the other is not that common, however. He described this communication as "episodic, random, and rare."

Finally, the fact that all DoDEA schools use the same curriculum helps to ensure that students won't fall behind during a move—even if they are in one DoDEA school in Germany on a Friday and enter another one in North Carolina the following Monday.

Supportive School Climates

DoDEA schools also build their school climate around the fact that students—and parents—are always on the move.

When a student comes in to a DoDEA school to register, the schools actually prefer that the student wait a day or two before coming to school, explains Patricia A. Cassiday, the former coordinator for counseling and psychological services for DoDEA.

That gives the teacher time to get a desk, books, and other materials ready for the student. It also gives the class a chance to prepare to welcome the new student. The scene is more of a "celebration instead of 'oh no, another student,'" Cassiday says.

An appointment with the school counselor is usually scheduled as soon as the student is enrolled.

In the classroom, teachers are trained to differentiate instruction to meet students' individual learning needs. Even though all DoDEA schools use the same curriculum, many students have still been in a variety of classrooms and through different experiences that could affect whether they are meeting the standards for their grade.

If a large deployment takes place, the school community will often hold a barbecue or some other event for the families. This is not only a way to recognize the servicemen and women, but also allows the schools to see how the spouses remaining behind are handling the transition. They might say they don't need support, Cassiday says, but they will attend something that is organized for their children.

Then, when a child is preparing to move on, the class or school offers some gesture to make the student feel as if they were appreciated. It can be as simple as a certificate, a T-shirt, or a pillowcase signed by all of student's classmates. It's a way to say, "thank you for being part of our school community," Cassiday says.

IMPACT AID

The federally funded Impact Aid program, first passed in 1950, was originally intended to compensate school districts when they lose a portion of their tax base because federal property—such as a military installation—is located within their boundaries and does not contribute to local tax revenues. In some cases, school districts are entirely located on a military base. In addition to losing property taxes, these districts might also lose sales taxes and other fees because military members have the option of shopping at stores (commissaries or exchanges) that don't charge taxes.

Impact Aid funds go directly to more than 1,300 school districts in the United States, which have considerable leeway in how they use them—purchasing textbooks or other resources, computers, utilities, and even hiring teachers. There is no formal requirement, however, to use these funds on behalf of military students. In addition, the program is not "forward funded," meaning that from year to year, school districts don't know how much Congress will appropriate for the program.

Over time, the program has been expanded to include other "federally connected" children, such as those living in subsidized housing, on tribal lands, or in national parks. That means less of the funding is used for military students.

Eligibility and Funding

In order to receive Impact Aid, at least 400 students or 3% of a school district's Average Daily Attendance must be federally connected. Districts receive more money from the program if their military students live on a base than if they live in the community.

All school districts seeking funds under the Impact Aid program must submit an application to the Department of Education no later than January 31 of each year. In order to prepare this application schools determine how many military students—or other federally connected students—they have by conducting a survey or by doing a parent's employment "source check." In both cases, for the application the district is required to collect and certify the child's name, age, grade, school, parent's name, and parent's work address (if civilian) or the rank and branch of service (for members of the uniformed services). These results are then used to fill out an Impact Aid application.

Although it is the district that applies for Impact Aid and not your individual school, it is important that you participate actively in this process. Some school administrators are reluctant to participate because they don't want to question parents about whether they are in the military. *Not doing so, however, means your district and school are losing federal money.*

In addition to basic payments, the program provides funds for construction-related expenses, including debt service. A discretionary Congressional grant program to supplement Impact Aid is also available to schools where at least 20% of the students are from military families. There are no application procedures for these supplemental funds. DoDEA, which is responsible for managing this program, contacts the eligible local education agencies.

Until 1970, the Impact Aid program was fully funded. But in the middle of that year, the funding was cut in half and has never been completely restored. The program is currently funded at 60% of the need.

Reform Proposals

Recent legislation focusing on Impact Aid reauthorization has focused on making sure federally impacted districts receive their payments in a "more timely fashion," increasing efficiency in the program and ensuring that districts don't receive less than in previous years. Early childhood education advocates have also recommended that the funds be used to provide pre-school programs.

Resources

The following organizations provide more detailed information on the Impact Aid program:

- The U.S. Department of Education provides official information on Impact Aid. http://www2.ed.gov/about/offices/list/oese/impactaid/index.html
- Military K–12 Partners, a DoDEA partnership program, provides a clear explanation of the application process and provides links to the forms required. http://www.militaryk12partners.dodea.edu/impact.cfm
- The Military Impacted Schools Association has a series of resources available on its website, including a video, a Power Point presentation, and a booklet. http://militaryimpactedschoolsassociation.org/
- The National Association of Federally Impacted Schools provides Impact Aid information under the"Basics" tab of its website. http://www.nafisdc.org/

CHAPTER 4

Deployment

Deployment refers to the assignment of an individual or a military unit to a location away from the home base for a task or a mission. A military service member can be deployed for a training exercise, peacekeeping mission, or to the middle of a war zone, so each deployment carries a unique set of circumstances that can affect the military member's children in different ways.

At a minimum, children experience a range of emotions and behaviors related to being separated from a parent for an extended period of time. That separation is compounded, however, by the fear that their parent could be in danger, could return with an injury, or might not return at all.

Some experts have observed that there are several emotional phases that families might also experience in relationship to the deployment cycle (Amen, Jellen, Merves, & Lee, 1988). For example, the pre-deployment phase can create tremendous anger and anxiety for children as they count down the days until their parent will be leaving. Alternately, some children might begin to withdraw from their deploying parent as they try to brace themselves for daily life without him or her. Deployment can leave a child feeling disorganized. The "reintegration" or reunion phase can be joyful, but also confusing–especially during a time of war–when a child realizes that his or her parent is somehow different than before the deployment.

You should be aware of the various–and sometimes unpredictable–ways that the deployment experience can affect military students' behavior in school and the attention they give to their academic work. You and your staff can create a warm and caring school climate that helps students through such difficult periods in their lives.

The Deployment Cycle

The cycle of deployment for a member of the military is described as having three main phases, each of which affect children in different ways:

- *Pre-deployment*—the notification that the military parent will be deployed
- *Deployment*—the period of time that the military parent is away
- *Post-deployment*—the return of the military parent, often also referred to as "reintegration"

THE WARS IN IRAQ AND AFGHANISTAN

The extended conflicts in Iraq and Afghanistan have led to a greater understanding of how children respond to the deployment of a parent. Since 2001, approximately two million military children have experienced a parent's deployment, according to DoDEA.

In addition, roughly 500,000 children—more than a third of all children with parents in the military—were born into military families since the beginning of those conflicts. For them, the potential that a parent will be deployed and put in harm's way has always been the norm. See the Research Highlights on Parental Deployment section at the end of this chapter.

MAJOR ISSUES RELATED TO DEPLOYMENT

The way a child responds to a parent's deployment can be unique to each child and the dynamics of his or her family. There are some overarching issues, however, that you should be aware of in your efforts to provide a stable environment for children during an unstable period in their lives.

Changing Roles in the Family: Possibly the most disruptive aspect of a parent's deployment is that the family members remaining behind must take on responsibilities that the deployed parent handled while he or she was home. For children, who tend to rely on routines and structure, this can be especially upsetting. Additional household chores or responsibilities, such as taking care of younger siblings, can shift to older children and affect whether they are getting their schoolwork done or maintaining their involvement in extracurricular activities. When a single parent is deployed, the upheaval can be even greater. Children might have to move in with family friends or relatives.

Block Leave: This is a period of time in the midst of a deployment—generally about 2 weeks—that a member of the military is allowed to return home to spend time with family members. Military students in your school may wish to stay home so they can spend time with their parent on leave. School districts with a large number of military families may already have a written policy outlining how many excused absences during this leave are allowed and the options students have for completing schoolwork at home during that time or making up missed assignments. If not, prepare in advance for these periods by crafting policies that allow students excused absences to reconnect with their military parent but that also keep students on pace with their schoolwork. Consult with teachers and parents about the performance of individual students. Are they caught up in class and generally responsible for turning in work completed at home? Or are they already behind and days

> I feel that the top priority is academic and I feel we are doing a pretty good job of that, but I think in order to do a better job of meeting the whole needs of the child I think there is still some room for improvement and partnership and collaboration.
>
> —Joel Tapia, associate principal,
> Heritage Elementary School, Chula Vista Elementary School District

out of school might make matters worse? In addition, parents may also expect that children should be excused from school on the day a parent leaves for a deployment or on the day the military parent's unit returns. These are other days to discuss in advance.

Financial Stress: If the parent being deployed is the one who paid all the bills, handled car maintenance, and managed other financial matters for the family, the parent left at home can be left completely unprepared for assuming these duties, especially if there will be limited communication between the parents during the deployment period. If the family recently moved before the deployment, the spouse at home might also still be looking for employment. In addition, increased child-care costs—which were not necessary when two parents were at home—can create an economic and sometimes unexpected burden on military families.

Relocating During a Deployment: When one parent is deployed, the other parent sometimes takes the children and moves in with family members or others who are able to provide support during this difficult time—even if it means moving across the country. While such a decision might provide more adults to care for the children, it can also add another disruption in the children's schooling and force them to adjust to another home and social environment. You may see some students leave your school for several months because their parent has deployed and the family has moved, or you may have new students enroll temporarily until their parent returns from deployment. These students may be especially anxious and vulnerable and may require special attention.

Multiple Deployments: One consequence of the fact that the wars in Iraq and Afghanistan have lasted so long is that many families have experienced multiple deployments. Just when a child gets used to having a parent home again, he or she is sent on another mission, and the relief associated with having a parent back in the home is not really experienced. "Multiple deployments" can also mean that a child has two parents in the military and both are deployed, or have back-to-back deployments. In this case, the child

4. Deployment

never has a stable home environment. One recent study, however, showed that some adolescents learn to cope better with each deployment. These students could possibly provide support and become role models for other students from military families.

Extended Deployments: Sometimes a deployment can last longer than expected, which can create extreme disappointment and anger in a family that is preparing to welcome home a service member at a specific time.

Well-Being of the Parent at Home: Studies have shown that one of the strongest predictors of emotional and behavioral problems for children during a deployment is how well the parent remaining with the child handles the stress that comes with being a military spouse. In addition, parents who use the support services available to them are more likely to have children that make it through the experience without significant negative outcomes.

Reintegration and Changing Relationships with the Deployed Parent: For younger and older children alike, a year or 18 months is a large period of time and one in which significant physical, social, and emotional development occurs. The way in which the child and the deployed parent interacted, communicated, and played together may be significantly different following the deployment period. The expectations of both the child and the parent may be unrealistic. The deployment may also cause negative changes in the relationship between the parents, which could turn what the child expected to be a happy reunion into a different one, filled with fear, anxiety, and resentment.

STRATEGIES FOR SCHOOLS

Here are suggestions for how schools can support both the academic and social-emotional well-being of children with deployed parents. Once again, the need to use multiple strategies depends on the number of military students in your school and the number of them that have parents who are deployed.

Attendance, Again: With the changes occurring at home, school may be the most stable place in a military child's life. While it's obvious that the child will want to be home on the day that his or her parent leaves for a deployment, regular attendance maintains a sense of predictability for the child. Monitor attendance data for increased absences or tardiness following a deployment. Perhaps the parent who got the child ready in the morning or drove the child to school is the one that is deployed and the transfer of those duties to the other parent or another adult is not going well. Encourage teachers to create incentives for regular attendance or to use "bell-ringer" activities at the beginning of the day to make students want to be in the classroom. For example, answering a "question of the day" before a specified time might earn a student extra credit. In addition, don't think that absences during the early grades are harmless. Even in preschool, regular attendance establishes patterns that are important for children to carry throughout their school years.

Using Organization Tools: A child with a deployed parent may be frequently distracted and disorganized. A student who used to turn in homework on time may now start missing assignments or losing them. Again, the parent who monitored homework completion or bought materials for out-of-class projects may be the one who is deployed. Organize the school day to allow students to complete homework at school or add an optional "before-school" period—perhaps in the cafeteria or a computer lab—that students can use to complete unfinished or missing work. Use student planners or other tools to help students keep track of assignments.

Increasing Communication with Parents: Be available to parents through phone and e-mail. Schedule a "morning coffee" or other opportunity for parents remaining at home with students to talk about their concerns during

4. Deployment

The following ideas come from the North Carolina Department of Public Instruction as part of the "NC Supports Military Children" section of its website. These suggestions offer ideas for both administrators and the teachers in your school.

- Refer students or families to military support organizations for information on deployment workshops, educational materials, or counseling services.
- Invite representatives from military family support organizations to PTA meetings to talk about separations and children.
- Encourage military families to attend deployment-focused programs.
- Encourage military parents to provide the school with the name of the unit they are assigned to and update the schools on deployment plans throughout the year. This allows the school to keep a confidential master list of students who have/will have parents deployed. This information helps teachers and counselors to be attuned to any emotional, behavioral, or academic changes that may occur with a student as a result of a parent being deployed.
- Facilitate deployment support groups for students whose parents or relatives are involved in a deployment.
- Put together a "Proud to be a Military Kid" bulletin board and encourage students to display pictures of military family members.

the deployment period. Alternately, schedule a meeting with students who have deployed parents to let them know you are supportive of their situation.

Staying Informed: Through communication with parents, school liaison officers, or other military base personnel, ask to be notified when a deployment, block leave, or reintegration is about to be announced or is about to begin. This will help you prepare for possible student absenteeism or other issues that could affect military students in your school.

Anti-War Comments: There may at times be students in your school who vocalize their opinions against war and other U.S. military actions. Teach students–and staff–to separate their feelings about the war from the way they treat military students in your school. Frequently reiterate that the military parents of your students are brave men and women who are serving their country. Following the suggestions in Chapter 2, "Mobility," regarding creating a military-friendly climate will help to encourage students to show respect, even if they disagree. It's harder to make hurtful remarks about someone when he or she is your friend.

Service Learning: Just as military parents are serving their country, students can learn to serve their community through integrated projects that combine academic skills with meeting local needs. Ask for input from military students in picking appropriate projects, such as sending letters or care packages to military members who are deployed. An Oceanside, California, student who was named a Military Child of the Year in 2011, for example, started a program in which baby showers are planned for military wives whose husbands are deployed. Such activities can also build students' confidence, sense of independence, and self-worth.

School Website: Use your school's website to show support for military parents who are deployed, and as a vehicle to keep parents informed about school events, students honored for outstanding performance, and other news. Many school districts now have secure portals for parents to track their children's grades and the completion of assignments. Opinions will differ among military families on whether it's helpful for deployed parents to use these services in order to monitor how their children are doing, or whether it creates additional stress on military members since they can't be of much help when they are half-way around the world and need to focus on life-or-death situations. It's possible that each family will need to determine the level of involvement that is right for their deployed family members.

Considering Test Times: If a unit is about to be deployed, or is about to return, talk with teachers about not scheduling tests around those times.

If testing dates are not flexible, make sure students and parents know well in advance when tests will be held. Plan extra review time or encourage study groups to keep students focused on preparing for the test. Think about creating incentives, such as class parties, to encourage students to attend the day of the test.

Support for the Parents: Think of ways to reduce the burdens on parents remaining at home with the child. Encourage teachers to limit long-term projects that require a lot of materials or work at home and to assign homework packets that can be completed over the course of the week instead of every night. Organize workshops for parents that focus on topics that might concern them the most, such as supporting their children through stressful periods, financial management, or community resources. Offer child care or activities for older students to make it easier for parents to attend.

Counting on Parent Volunteers: Many school PTAs or other parent associations have "caring committees" that provide meals, organize play dates, or take on other responsibilities for families in times of need, such as when a parent is ill, or after the birth of a baby. Encourage these committees to offer their assistance during deployment periods as well. They can organize rides to after-school activities, sports, or study sessions for children with deployed parents. It's important that students stay involved in what they enjoy, but it's likely that the parent at home may feel overwhelmed and can't do it all alone.

Monitoring Nutrition: Disruption and stress at home can mean that children aren't eating properly. Participate in the National School Breakfast Program to ensure that students have a healthy meal before beginning their school day. Make sure that military parents are informed about how to apply for the free or reduced-price lunch program.

Making Students Feel Special: A child may sometimes feel ignored when his or her parents are preparing for and coping with a deployment. Perhaps schedule a special school event, before or during a deployment, to give students something to look forward to. In addition, when opportunities arise, tell military students that you are proud of them and their parents.

Avoiding Relocation: As mentioned, families sometimes choose to move closer to relatives or close friends when one parent is deployed—even if it means taking their children out of school. Explore options for avoiding such moves, as they will further disrupt students' education. If students feel welcome and wanted in your school, and if parents have a support network in their community, they may feel better able to weather the deployment period without uprooting again.

4. Deployment

Principal Spotlight: Pat Kurtz, principal of
Santa Margarita Elementary School, Oceanside, California

As the principal of a school where almost 100% of the students have parents in the military, Pat Kurtz uses multiple approaches to help students handle the changes that are often occurring in their home lives. Santa Margarita Elementary is located on Marine Corps Base Camp Pendleton.

But some of the practices, Kurtz says, would be beneficial for any school interested in providing children with positive ways to handle the challenges they face.

Photo by
Rashell Parkhurst

Instead of organizing support groups just for children who have a deployed parent, Kurtz has found greater success with what she calls "friendship groups" and "leadership groups." These consist of about four students—two of which clearly need some help with social skills and another two that she says "are a little bit quiet" and might need some help forming relationships. The friendship groups refer to those gatherings of students in K–2 and the leadership groups are for students in grades 3–5.

This combination, which is created in collaboration between Kurtz and the teachers, seems to work well, she said. With their parents' permission, the students are excused from class to meet in their groups and just talk about whatever topics might be on their minds.

Kurtz and her staff also pay close attention to how children interact on the playground—a setting, she says, that often sparks aggressive behavior or other social and emotional difficulties for students.

"Ninety percent of my referrals are from the playground," she says, adding that for a lot of students, especially those on the autism spectrum, "the playground is not their friend."

First, she provided a high level of training to the playground supervisors, making sure they know conflict resolution techniques and stay involved in what is happening during recess.

Secondly, she opened up what she calls a Lunch Recess Options (LRO) room, located just off the playground, and filled it with computers, games, art supplies, and other materials that students can use if they need a retreat from the playground environment. Some students also use the room, which is supervised, to complete homework. Kurtz used an endowment from the architect for the recently renovated school to purchase a generous supply of Legos. Again, consulting with teachers and the school's special education aide, Kurtz has identified which students have priority to be in the LRO.

Whenever possible, Kurtz also takes advantage of funding opportunities for additional play structures and games—items that she believes help to reduce the conflicts that can flare up on the playground when children are waiting too long for a certain piece of equipment.

For students that have to be suspended, Kurtz has tried to be sensitive to the job requirements of military parents. Instead of springing on them that they will have to take a day off from work to stay home with their child, she allows the parents to choose a day that is more convenient for them.

"You respect the fact that they have a very demanding situation and a very demanding job," she says.

Kurtz is not sure how to put a name on another practice that has emerged at her school, but it is one that has made a difference for many of the young military mothers at Santa Margarita. There are some teachers at the school, along with Kurtz, who have taken an informal role as surrogate grandmothers to some of the military children. Having an older woman to provide support and mentoring to the younger women, who become "temporary single parents," has been a powerful tool, Kurtz says.

While it's not the kind of practice that Kurtz would know how to recommend to other school leaders, she says it is a dynamic that has been successful at her school.

"There is something about being a teacher and being a guide to a parent at the same time," she says.

Ultimately, Kurtz says she would like to see a young mothers' support group at her school—something that she believes would be more successful than asking them to come to a parenting class.

Several teachers at Santa Margarita have also honored students' military parents by creating "Hero Walls" in their classrooms—displays that include photos of the students' family members and perhaps information on where they have traveled and when they are expected to return.

4. Deployment

A Hero Wall at Santa Margarita Elementary

Photo by
Rashell Parkhurst

She has found, however, that this practice has been more successful with students in the primary grades than with older elementary school students who might be tired of talking about another deployment.

Finally, Kurtz has used the "Tell Me a Story" program from the Military Child Education Coalition to give parents and children at her school a chance to talk about some of the experiences that they might confront as a military family—such as loss, moving to a new place, separation, or trying to fit in.

Families gather for a "Tell Me a Story" event at the school, in which they hear the selected book and then break up into small groups for a discussion and activities with a facilitator. At the end of the evening, families receive their own copy of the book.

Kurtz finds that the gathering works best with no more than about 45 people. While the program was designed to support military families, it's another practice that she believes could also be successful at a school without a lot of military children. Not only does the activity help explain difficult feelings, but it also helps build literacy skills.

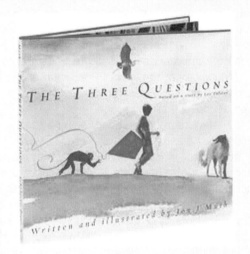

The Three Questions by John Muth is one of the books used in the Tell Me a Story program.

RESEARCH HIGHLIGHTS ON PARENTAL DEPLOYMENT

- Studies show that since the beginning of the Iraq war, the demand for psychiatric services by military children has doubled to two million mental health outpatient visits (Gorman, Eide, & Hisle-Gorman, 2010). Psychiatric hospitalizations of military children for severe problems, including suicidal behaviors, have increased by 50%.
- A study by the RAND Corporation–involving 1,500 children who attended a summer camp program offered by the National Military Family Association–found that longer periods of deployment are associated with more social and emotional problems for children (Richardson et al., 2011). The effects of deployment also vary by children's age and gender. Older rather than younger students were more likely to have problems in school and with their peers during deployment. Girls were more likely than boys to have problems related to their parent returning from duty.
- Children as young as 3 can experience emotional and behavioral issues related to a parent's deployment, according to a 2008 study by Molinda M. Chartrand from the Boston University School of Public Health. This finding has implications for elementary schools and those that operate preschool or other early-childhood programs. When compared to children without deployed parents, preschoolers with a parent deployed during wartime had higher rates of internalizing behaviors, such as anxiety, depression, and withdrawal, and externalizing behaviors, such as attention difficulties and aggression.
- Alyssa J. Mansfield, formerly of the University of North Carolina at Chapel Hill and now with the National Center for Posttraumatic Stress Disorder in Honolulu, found that children with a parent who was deployed in Operation Iraqi Freedom and Operation Enduring Freedom for longer periods were more likely to receive a diagnosis of a mental health problem than children whose parents did not deploy (Mansfield et al., 2011). The study included 307,520 children, of whom 16.7% had a mental health diagnosis. More than 62% of parents were deployed at least once during the period, for an average of 11 months. The study found that mental health problems were more likely among children who had a parent deployed at least once to Iraq or Afghanistan. The likelihood of a mental health diagnosis increased with longer deployments. Among the 6,579 mental health diagnoses observed, the most common were acute stress reaction and adjustment disorders, depressive disorders, and behavioral disorders.

4. Deployment

RESOURCES

Listed below are organizations, programs, and publications that can increase school leaders' understanding of the issues military families face when a parent is deployed.

Educator's Guide to the Military Child During Deployment: This document was sponsored by the Educational Opportunities Directorate of the Department of Defense in collaboration with Marleen Wong, one of the authors of this book. http://militarystudent.whhive.com/Content/Media/File/MISA/educators_guide.pdf

Military-Connected Students and Public School Attendance Policies: This report from the Military Child Education Coalition provides an informative section on the ways some states handle attendance issues related to block leave or other events related to deployment. http://www.militarychild.org/public/upload/files/SchoolAttendancePoliciesFINAL.pdf

Military Deployment and Families: This audio is part of the Healthy Children initiative of the American Academy of Pediatrics. http://www.healthychildren.org/English/family-life/family-dynamics/pages/Military-Deployment-and-Families.aspx

SOFAR: Strategic Outreach to Families of All Reservists (SOFAR) aids families of Army Reservists and members of the National Guard. SOFAR is a mental health project that provides free psychological support, psychotherapy, psychoeducation, and prevention services to extended family members before and after a deployment. http://www.sofarusa.org/index.html

Young Children on the Homefront: Family Stories, Family Strengths: This DVD is useful to teachers who work with young children. Part of the Zero to Three organization's Coming Together Around Military Families initiative, the DVD provides tips and strategies for supporting children before, during, and after a deployment. Themes include Staying Connected, Stress and Behavior, Routines and Reunification. http://www.zerotothree.org/about-us/funded-projects/military-families/children-on-the-homefront.html. Zero to Three also provides other tools appropriate for young children. "More Changes? Are You Kidding Me?" is a short two-page flier about reintegration. And *Home Again* is a board book for young children, parents, and caregivers about the reunification experience.

Ready, Set, Go!: This manual and training opportunity is part of Operation: Military Kids, the U.S. Army's effort to partner with community organizations to support military families during deployment. A wide variety of other resources and links are also available at this site. http://www.4-hmilitarypartnerships.org/DesktopDefault.aspx?tabid=127

Surviving Deployment.com: This site provides ideas for activities, links to other resources, and helpful articles, such as "Helping Children Handle Deployments." It is written for parents, but useful for educators as well. http://www.survivingdeployment.com/articles.html

How to Prepare Our Children and Stay Involved in Their Education During Deployment: This booklet from the Military Child Education Coalition offers suggestions for both parents and educators and provides insight into some of the thoughts and feelings that students might have surrounding the deployment of a parent. http://www.militarychild.org/files/pdfs/DeploymentBooklet.pdf

Helping Children Cope with the Challenges of War and Terrorism: This workbook provides activities for adults and children to identify, understand, and cope with their feelings. http://www.7-dippity.com/other/UWA_war_book.pdf

Talk, Listen, Connect: This is an initiative of Sesame Workshop, the organization behind *Sesame Street.* In partnership with Walmart and The New York Office of Mental Health, the effort focuses on helping young children of military members cope with feelings, challenges and concerns related to deployment. The site offers videos featuring popular Muppet characters as well as other materials. http://www.sesameworkshop.org/what-we-do/our-work/reaching-out-to-military-families-6-detail.html

The Coming Home Project: Based in San Francisco, this organization offers a speakers' bureau, training videos, and other resources for organizations, such as churches and schools, that serve veterans returning from Iraq and Afghanistan and their families. It also provides training materials for professionals on issues related to deployment and reintegration, such as marital problems. http://www.cominghomeproject.net/community

4. Deployment

District Spotlight: Escondido Union School District

Located southeast of Marine Corps Base Camp Pendleton, the Escondido Union School District does not have easy access to programs and services meant for military families. That's why the district has made it a priority to bring services into the school buildings to make it more convenient for children and families to benefit from counseling, support, and other types of programs.

"This is their home, but the bases are so far away," Kimberly Israel says about military families in the district. "We can't expect them to take advantage of a counseling service that is 30 minutes away."

Israel is the project director for the district's CARE (Collaborative Agency Resources for Escondido) Youth Project, a partnership with agencies such as the County of San Diego Health and Human Services Agency and the county's Probation Department. By memorandums of understanding with the partners, the schools are able to offer programs ranging from alcohol and drug prevention and a student leadership program, to school-based mental health counseling and mobile dental services.

Together, Growing a
Safer and Healthier Escondido

The district is also committed to having social workers in the schools and funds more of these positions than most of its neighboring districts. Tailoring the services to meet the needs at each school involves ongoing communication between the district and local principals.

"In our district, we are constantly in dialogue with our principals on developing a system of services," Israel says.

For example, some principals choose to send students who have gotten in trouble to a "choices and challenges" class instead of suspending them. If that is their approach, "we have to make sure we have choice-making classes available," Israel says.

The district has also increased efforts to educate principals about the military families in their school communities and the needs of these families—a student demographic that previously didn't receive a lot of direct attention, Israel says.

Surveys of parents and results from the California Healthy Kids Survey—which displayed data on military and nonmilitary students—is now creating greater awareness among principals and other staff about the need to support military students and the changes that their families might be experiencing.

"We want to open more doors for those families," Israel says.

CHAPTER 5

Traumatic Experiences

As a school administrator, you have encountered and will continue to find situations in which painful experiences involving your students impact your school community. As a leader in your school and district, your views on how to respond to such issues can set the tone for how the rest of your staff handles them. Trauma, such as a parent's death, illness, or injury, can affect any child in your school. In this chapter, we focus on the types of traumatic experiences that are more common among military families.

School leaders often make remarks about educating the whole child. But they may have differing views on their role in helping students through the troubling—and even traumatic—events in their lives.

We have organized these views into three main philosophies, described below.

First, you may feel that the school only has an academic mission, and that family tragedies or a child's personal problems should be tended to primarily by outside counselors, faith-based organizations, or other trained professionals—it's not the school's job.

Second, you may believe that it is important to have counselors, nurses, or other support personnel on hand to address children's nonacademic needs, but that teachers should not get involved and that students' personal troubles should remain private as much as possible.

Finally, you may consider it appropriate for your school to act as a supportive community when families are in need—whether there is an illness, a financial hardship, or even a death—recognizing that for children to be academically successful, schools must often address other physical, mental, or emotional problems that are getting in the way.

Whichever of these three categories you are in will determine how your school approaches many of the issues affecting military students—which can include exposure to uncomfortable topics and frightening situations and events that civilian children typically don't have to worry about.

If you count yourself among those administrators in the first or second categories, realize that the issues children face outside of school will still affect how they function in the classroom. If you put yourself in the third category, recognize that your staff and teachers may still need your leadership and training in how to:

- recognize the signs that children are struggling
- support social-emotional development in the classroom
- build a sense of community and resiliency among your students
- know when to refer a child to school psychologists or social workers

MILITARY CHILDREN AND TRAUMA

As mentioned in Chapter 4, simply being separated from a parent for an extended period can be more upsetting for some children than it is for others, depending on a variety of factors. For some military children, one more school transfer—especially if previous moves were problematic—may be the event that sparks emotions and behavior that are more serious than just being disappointed and angry.

Living with fear that a parent—or another relative—serving in the military is in danger can create stress for a child to the point where it significantly affects his or her ability to function in the school environment.

In addition, members of the military often return from a wartime deployment changed by the experience. The effects can be physical—as with an injury—or psychological. Either way, they can impact a service member's parenting ability.

As an administrator of a school serving military children, you should be prepared for these possibilities, aware of military and community resources available to returning veterans and their families, and equipped with strategies that can support children coping with trauma.

Your school can be a refuge and a welcome distraction for military families if you and others in your school are prepared in advance to respond to these issues and recognize that you can play a part in helping the child get through such difficult times.

WOUNDED PARENTS

Many thousands of children have had a parent wounded in action since the beginning of the wars in Iraq and Afghanistan.

Some injuries are serious enough to require rehabilitation and could extend the time that a child is separated from his or her parent. A debilitating injury can dramatically affect that parent's relationship with the child and can continue to create shifting responsibilities in the home, even though the deployed parent has returned.

But sometimes the damage is invisible, as is the case with traumatic brain injury (TBI), a condition in which a violent blow to the head causes a collision between the brain and the inside of the skull. The rampant use of improvised explosive devices (IEDs) by enemy forces in Iraq and Afghanistan has resulted in many veterans returning with TBI, which is hard to diagnose, but can have lasting effects.

To a child, especially a young child, his or her parent may appear the same. But the symptoms, such as headaches, concentration problems, mood changes, depression, anxiety, and fatigue can significantly interfere with family relationships.

Even if a parent returns from battle without a physical injury, many suffer from psychological wounds that increase stress in the home, damage the relationship between the parent and the child, and can further affect how that child is performing in your school. Depression, suicidal thoughts, post-traumatic stress disorder (PTSD), substance abuse, and other mental health issues are not uncommon among returning veterans.

Children, as a result, can suffer just as much as their parents. Parents with PTSD may avoid certain subjects or situations that are reminders of the violence or trauma they experienced. They may constantly appear on edge or about to explode with anger, and even re-experience traumatic events as if they were still on the battlefield.

All of these behaviors are upsetting for children and affect their relationship with their parent. They may feel that they are the cause of reminding their parent of the trauma. They might feel as if their parent doesn't love them, and they too may begin to exhibit symptoms that are similar to those of their parents. Some experts describe the effects of trauma on the soldiers' spouses and children as "secondary traumatization."

Some studies have also shown that child maltreatment—including physical, emotional, or sexual abuse—increased among military families as more troops were being sent into Iraq and Afghanistan.

Don't assume that because a military parent has been deployed or was injured in combat that he or she is going to become violent, suicidal, or display other symptoms of serious mental illness. But in some cases, a parent's war wounds—both physical and psychological—can help to explain changes in a student's behavior at school.

THE DEATH OF A PARENT

The death of a student's parent affects not only that family but also your school community. Because the military has specific procedures for notifying and caring for family members upon the death of a service member, you may not be among the first to know if the parent of a child in your school has died in combat or as a result of another military action.

This is one reason why it is essential for schools to have a plan in place for responding to a parent's death—whether the parent is in the military or not.

5. Traumatic Experiences

In the event of a parent's death, the way your school responds is not only significant for the child who has lost a parent, but will also serve as an example to students and other members of the community, many of whom will be struggling with how to talk to the student and be supportive when he or she returns to the classroom.

Often, when someone's relative dies, the people around them don't say anything because they don't want to offend anyone, they are afraid of saying the wrong thing or triggering an emotional reaction, or they don't want to appear intrusive. But children spend so much of their lives in school that pretending nothing has happened is unrealistic and the silence could hinder how that child learns to adapt to his or her loss.

MAJOR ISSUES RELATED TO TRAUMA

Military families often face complex and complicated issues when coping with a war-related tragedy. Trauma and intense stress at home can seriously distract children from their responsibilities at school and impact their success in the classroom. The following are topics that you should be prepared to address.

Special Education Referrals: Children often do not have the words to explain why are they are acting out, having tantrums, or not concentrating in class. Maybe their parents argue at home, they are worried about whether their parents have enough money, or a parent came back from Iraq in a wheelchair. They may not even understand the range of emotions they are feeling. Behavioral, emotional, and learning problems, however, are often considered reasons to refer a child for special education or a 504 plan, especially if teachers don't know that the child's difficulties are related to being in a military family. If your school serves military children, make sure this is considered when reviewing special education referrals.

Effects on the Other Parent: If a military parent returns from battle with a serious injury, the other parent may be so traumatized by that experience— or busy with the person's treatment and recovery—that he or she cannot give appropriate care and attention to the child. The same could be the case with PTSD or other mental health problems. Furthermore, if one parent has died, the surviving parent may not be able to carry on with routines that allow the child to do well in school.

Another Move: If a parent is injured, the family may be faced with relocating again in order for that parent to receive appropriate medical care or rehabilitation. If a military parent dies, this could also precipitate another move so the surviving parent can be closer to friends and extended family members. This creates another community and school transition for the child that was not expected in the normal course of being part of a military family. If your school is located near a large military medical facility, you may have students in your school who are there temporarily while an injured parent is being treated. These students also may present unique challenges in your school.

Loss of Military Identity: Even when military children attend regular public schools, they have grown up in a military community and lifestyle that is part of how they identify themselves. Their close friends are probably other military children, and they perhaps attend recreation or summer programs especially designed for children of military members. If a child's parent doesn't return to active duty following an injury, or if a military parent dies, that child's lifestyle and routine could change abruptly because they would no longer be eligible for some of the same programs. This is another level of loss and transition for a military child.

Perceptions of the Military Parent: If the school community views the military member as a hero and as someone who has performed a valuable service to the country, the child will share in that sense of pride and appreciation. But if a death or injury was self-inflicted or involves substance abuse, the community is likely to treat the family differently and the child may feel shame.

Disengagement in Schoolwork: If a parent is seriously injured, has died, or is experiencing significant trauma following reintegration, a child may feel that everything else in life is insignificant compared to the issues being confronted at home. Telling a child to focus on schoolwork may only generate resentment and make him or her think that you don't care. Furthermore, the child may be reluctant to attend school in hopes of avoiding questions about what is happening at home.

5. Traumatic Experiences

Trauma-sensitive schools acknowledge the prevalence of traumatic occurrence in students' lives and create a flexible framework that provides universal supports, is sensitive to unique needs of students, and is mindful of avoiding re-traumatization.

—From "Creating Trauma-Sensitive Schools," a PowerPoint presentation from the Wisconsin Department of Public Instruction.

The presentation is available at: http://dpi.wi.gov/sspw/mhtrauma.html

STRATEGIES FOR SCHOOLS

A military student may face one or more of the major issues described above. Depending on the type of trauma or tragedy the child is experiencing—and how it is impacting the child in your school—your staff may be involved in responding during the first few hours or days, months later, or on an ongoing basis.

Encourage teachers and counselors to find balance between maintaining a sense of routine for the child at school and being sensitive to their specific situation, their need for flexibility, and a gradual return to a normal schedule.

Below are suggestions for creating a school environment that is sensitive to military students experiencing high levels of grief or trauma.

Maintaining Routine: If a student's parent has died or been seriously injured, teachers should allow time for discussion and answering questions, providing only the facts that they know. Don't ignore that something tragic has occurred. But you should also encourage teachers to return to their normal classroom routine as soon as possible to give that student—and the whole class—a sense of security and stability.

Involving Your School Nurse: Children experiencing depression or wanting to avoid certain social situations often end up in the nurse's office complaining of stomach problems or a headache. Consult frequently with the school nurse to determine whether he or she has repeat visitors who are military children. This could indicate that the child needs more support in the classroom, is feeling ostracized by peers, or that a conversation with the parent is necessary.

School Displays: A bulletin board, banner, or other display honoring members of the military that previously made a child feel welcomed and appreciated may now only serve as a disturbing reminder of what his or her parent and family has been through. Discuss with the child whether it should be removed or replaced with something else.

Planning for the Unexpected: A child that is experiencing trauma or fear can become agitated by changes in the daily routine, such as a fire drill, a large assembly or visitors to the school. Discuss these situations with teachers and pupil personnel to determine whether it would be helpful to inform students of changes in the routine ahead of time.

Allowing Breaks: While routine is good, students experiencing extreme stress or trauma may also need opportunities to excuse themselves from class during the school day to speak to a counselor, or to block out conversations or topics that are reminding them of upsetting events at home. Make sure teachers allow such breaks. Some schools also create a "safe" or "quiet" room as a retreat for students, perhaps staffed by a trusted volunteer or counselor.

Online Learning: If a child is missing school because of a parent's injury, a death, or other trauma in the home, explore options for allowing the student to complete assignments using a home computer or earn credits through online homeschooling.

Staff Development: Provide your teachers with training on how to recognize the signs that students are experiencing trauma, to understand how chronic stress affects learning, and to avoid conflicts with students or triggers that make them shut down and refuse to do their schoolwork.

Memorials: When a child dies, school communities often hold a memorial service to give students a chance to express their feelings and thoughts about the student. If the family agrees, the same can be held for a military parent who has died. Whether the school honors the parent's service to his or her country can have a significant impact on the family's continuing relationship with your school. If the family doesn't want this, students can still send cards or letters to the family showing their support.

Partnering with Mental Health Services: Having partnerships with outside mental health agencies can benefit students in time of need. But studies have also shown that when schools provide opportunities for students to seek help from someone as part of their regular school day, they will use those services. If your school has a nurse's office, consider adding a mental health professional to the staff—even if the person only works part-time—so students can have someone to talk to if they feel the need.

Daily Report Cards: This strategy is sometimes used to communicate with parents if they have a child who has problems coping through the school day or to encourage improvement in behavior. Such an approach could be customized for a child that has experienced significant trauma and is having difficulty completing assignments, getting along with peers, or following school rules. This process may become a new routine for the child that they depend on and that helps him or her set goals and work through strong emotions.

Contacting the Next School: If a military child is about to move again, administrators or counselors at the child's next school should be made aware if the child has been dealing with experiences that can drastically affect his or her progress in school and their future beyond graduation. If you don't know where the child is headed, ask the parents to let you know as soon as possible. In spite of how busy or even traumatized the family is, they may appreciate your inquiry and respond.

Finding Meaning: It's normal for children to think only about how a tragedy, a parent's illness, or some other challenging situation affects them and their normal routine. But some children also live through such events to help others or to raise awareness about a particular need. Help children understand that they are not alone, that there are organizations of military children who have been through similar circumstances, and that they too can provide strength and understanding for others facing difficult times.

RESOURCES

The following resources and organizations provide advice and information on handling issues of grief and trauma in school. While some are focused specifically on military children, others are more general. Some of these may also be useful to the teachers and other staff members in your school who have daily contact with students.

The National Child Traumatic Stress Network: This site explains types of trauma and provides a section focusing specifically on military children and families as well as a section geared toward educators. http://www.nctsnet.org/

Child Trauma Toolkit for Educators: From the National Child Traumatic Stress Network, this resource explains the psychological and behavioral impacts of trauma at each stage of childhood, from the preschool years through high school. http://www.nctsnet.org/nctsn_assets/pdfs/Child_Trauma_Toolkit_Final.pdf

SOS Signs of Suicide: This prevention program from Screening for Mental Health is designed specifically for middle and high school students. It teaches students how to identify depression and other symptoms within themselves or their friends that could lead to suicide or suicide attempts. The program uses the ACT® technique, which stands for Acknowledge, Care and Tell. Newer materials in the program include a DVD to be used in the high school program. *SOS Friends for Life* features true stories of three teenagers who struggled with mental health issues. It also provides students with instructions for how to recognize signs of distress in themselves or a friend and how to respond effectively. This resource can be shared with particular students or used as part of wider suicide prevention efforts in your school. http://mentalhealthscreening.org/programs/youth-prevention-programs/sos/default.aspx

Talk, Listen, Connect: This is an initiative of Sesame Workshop, the organization behind *Sesame Street*. In partnership with Walmart and the New York Office of Mental Health, the effort includes videos and other materials focused on helping young children of military members cope with grief. http://www.sesameworkshop.org/what-we-do/our-work/reaching-out-to-military-families-6-detail.html

Child's Grief Education Association: This organization's website includes a section on military families in addition to useful basic advice on helping children deal with grief and loss. http://www.childgrief.org/childgrief.htm

Tragedy Assistance Program for Survivors: This organization provides around-the-clock services for military families, such as emotional support, crisis intervention, grief and trauma resources, and "Good Grief" camps for children. http://www.taps.org/

When Death Impacts Your School: This article from The Dougy Center: The National Center for Grieving Children and Families gives teachers specific suggestions on how to communicate with grieving students in the classroom, including what and what not to say. http://www.dougy.org/grief-resources/death-impacts-your-school/

Resources for Wounded or Injured Service Members and Their Families: This factsheet from the National Military Family Association provides basic definitions and information on procedures related to wounded warriors. http://support.militaryfamily.org/site/DocServer/Wounded_Servicemember7-06.pdf?docID=6703

When a Child's Parent has PTSD: The National Center for PTSD at the U.S. Department of Veterans Affairs provides useful information on how a parent's PTSD can affect their child. http://www.ptsd.va.gov/public/pages/children-of-vets-adults-ptsd.asp

The National Institute for Trauma and Loss in Children provides direct services to traumatized children and families as well as resource materials. The website has a series of podcasts featuring professionals who have worked with military families regarding deployment and other experiences. http://www.starrtraining.org/tlc

Trauma Faced by Children of Military Families: What Every Policy-maker Should Know: This is available on the National Center for Children in Poverty website. It provides a simple overview of the de-mographics of military children, many of the challenges they face, key research findings related to deployment and mental health, as well as some of the resources designed to help military families. http://www. nccp.org/publications/pub_938.html

Support for Students Exposed to Trauma: The SSET Program: De-veloped by researchers at RAND in collaboration with Marleen Wong, an Assistant Dean in the USC School of Social Work, this manual can be used by teachers and provides lesson plans, materials, and worksheets for use in a group setting. The program was not originally intended for military children, but can apply to many of the situations they might be facing. http://www. rand.org/pubs/research_briefs/RB9443-1/index1.html

---

Promising Practice Spotlight: Heroes' Tree

The Heroes' Tree is an initiative that involves the community in recognizing and honoring both living and deceased members of the armed forces. Founded by authors Stephanie Pickup and Marlene Lee, the project is a partnership led by the Military Family Research Institute (MFRI) at Purdue University.

Heroes' Trees are similar to Christmas trees, but are adorned with handmade ornaments featuring photographs of military service members or drawings that represent service members. While the trees have been placed in local libraries in Indiana, schools are also appropriate places for the trees—allowing students to pay tribute to heroes in their lives and to learn about the role of the military in U.S. history.

Example of a Heroes' Tree ornament

The project is noncontroversial and all-inclusive, explains Kathy Broniarczyk, the director of outreach for MFRI, because the servicemen and women honored don't have to be current members of the military. They can be someone's grandfather or uncle or a long-deceased relative who served in a past war. The project raises awareness of the sacrifices that have been made by service members and their families and creates opportunities for a variety of learning experiences for students.

In addition to the literal trees placed in libraries and other places where members of the community gather, a Virtual Heroes' Tree has also been created to serve as a web-based extension of the project, allowing anyone to take part in viewing information on the members being honored and to learn about their service.

In its resource guide, the MFRI has also compiled an extensive list of ideas for school and community programs involving children and youth. Many would be appropriate for school service-learning projects. They include:

- Taking a graveyard exploration trip and writing down information from a tombstone of a deceased veteran
- Using library genealogy resources to investigate and collect biographical information on living local relatives of the veteran, and then interviewing the relatives to learn more about the service member's military experience
- Creating family trees that make note of any relatives who served in the armed forces or in military branches of other countries
- Identifying the needs of veterans in local nursing homes and Veterans' Administration hospitals and brainstorming ideas for helping them
- Interviewing veterans about their military service, any memorable stories, their job in the military, and whether they served during a war

To access the resource guide, view the Virtual Heroes' Tree and learn more about the Heroes' Tree program, visit: http://www.cfs.purdue.edu/mfri/public/oht/Default.aspx.

5. Traumatic Experiences

CHAPTER 6

Using Data to Improve School Climate for Military Students

Understanding and using data has become an integral part of a school administrator's job. School leaders are expected to make decisions regarding student instruction, policies, discipline, teacher evaluation–and just about everything else within their job description–based on data. But if you don't even know how many military students are in your school, or some of the issues they and their families are struggling with, you can't accurately target their needs or implement practices that can make their experiences in your school more positive.

In previous sections, we have alluded to the need for data specifically on this population. And your school may already be collecting some information in order to receive Impact Aid funds. But here we take a more thorough look at what you might want to know and how you can use the information to improve school climate and student outcomes.

SCHOOL SAFETY AND CLIMATE SURVEYS

The environment in which students go to school every day has been found to have an effect on how they learn. In addition, there are a variety of non-academic issues that can influence student achievement, such as supportive relationships, exposure to drugs and alcohol, bullying, sex, and mental health.

To better understand these factors, many states already collect information on school climate and the risk and resiliency factors that are part of students' lives. These anonymous surveys can help to identify which groups of students are having a harder time coping with the challenges of social relationships, feel pressured by peers to try drugs or alcohol, or have concerns about their safety.

Important Points to Consider

When conducting school climate or youth risk and behavior surveys, keep these things in mind:

- *Use language appropriate to your audience.* Make surveys available in the language(s) spoken by families in your school. Avoid jargon.
- *Clarify that school is the context in focus.* Use terms such as "on school grounds" or "during school hours."
- *Include concrete behaviors.* Terms such as "violence," "aggression," and even "bullying" can be understood differently. Use concrete terms such as "a student cursed at me," "pushed me," "kicked me," "spread bad rumors about me," etc.
- *Select appropriate time frame.* Clarify the time frames in which events occur—"ever," "in the past school year," "in the past 30 days," "today," etc.
- *Select appropriate response scale.* Use a scale that allows respondents to display whether or not something has occurred and how often.
- *Create indices when appropriate.* Asking several questions regarding the same topic can capture more complex and rich data. These results are later combined to create an index or a composite score.
- *Include validity checks.* A question such as "I am reading and responding to this survey carefully" can help determine whether the respondent is paying attention.
- *Consider attractive and alternative visual formats.* Younger students may especially respond to colorful surveys using cartoon figures and illustrations.

Educators, however, don't receive data on their individual school, and if they do, they often don't know what to do with it to make specific changes that will improve outcomes for students at their schools. In addition, until now, schools have not been looking at how military students are faring on these health risk and behavior surveys and whether they are similar or different in these areas compared with their peers. As a result, many of these students' needs have been left unidentified.

6. Using Data to Improve Schools

A MILITARY SURVEY MODULE FOR CALIFORNIA

A major component of the Building Capacity project at USC was the creation and administration of a new "module" for military students that was added to the California Healthy Kids Survey (CHKS). The survey provides policymakers and educators with valuable information on school climate and student trends regarding exposure to drugs, violence, bullying, and other risk and protective factors that affect student learning. The Military-Connected School Module was developed by USC researchers in partnership with eight military-connected school districts near San Diego and WestEd, the research and service agency that administers the CHKS for the California Department of Education.

The new supplemental module is the first effort to better understand how military-connected children are doing in the public schools that they attend, and allows schools to gather feedback from military children about their experiences in civilian schools. The questions provide important insight into whether they perceive their schools to be friendly and supportive, and if they think their families are respected by the adults in their schools.

Parallel survey questionnaires for both staff (the California School Climate Survey) and parents (the California School Parent Survey) in the same schools were also administered to gather the potential multiple perspectives and solutions that could improve the ways schools serve students from military families. While the module was used in those districts as part of the Building Capacity project, it was available to any school in the state.

In the tables below, we provide examples of the topic areas and types of questions that appear in both the CHKS "core" and the CHKS military module. We include examples from the surveys given to students, school staff, and parents.

Examples of Modules and Questions from the California Healthy Kids Survey (CHKS) for High School Students

Topics	Examples of Questions
Module A: Core	
1. Background Info	What is your gender?; Grade?
2. School Connectedness and Participation	I feel close to people at this school.
3. Adult Support and Participation in Community	Outside of my home and school, there is an adult who really cares about me.
4. Eating Habits	Did you eat breakfast today?
5. Alcohol, Tobacco, Marijuana, & Other Drug Use	During your *life*, how many times have you used or tried a whole cigarette?

Topics	Examples of Questions
6. Violence, Safety, Harassment & Bullying	During the *past 12 months*, how many times on school property have you been pushed, shoved, slapped, hit, or kicked by someone who wasn't just kidding around?
7. Sadness, Suicidal Thoughts	During the *past 12 months*, did you ever seriously consider attempting suicide?
8. Betting/ Gambling	During the *past 12 months*, how often have you bet/ gambled, even casually, for money or valuables in card or dice games (such as poker, blackjack, or craps)?

Military Module

1. Military Connectedness	Who in your family is *currently* in the military?
2. Personal and Family Strengths	My family is very close and we support each other; I am more independent than many of my friends.
3. School Experiences	Other students in school do not really understand my family life; I have a hard time making friends because I have to change schools often.
4. Mood and Affect	In the *last 30 days*, how often did you feel full of energy?
5. Experiences as a Military Student	In the *last 5 years*, how many times did you change your school because your family had to move?

Additional Available Modules

Resilience Supplemental

AOD (Alcohol and Other Drugs), Violence, & Suicide

Tobacco

Physical Health & Nutrition

Sexual Behavior

District Afterschool (DASM)

Gang Risk Awareness

Service Learning

Closing the Achievement Gap (CTAG)

Safe and Supportive Schools (S3)

After-school Program

Building Healthy Communities (BHC)

School Health Center

California Student Survey (CSS)

6. Using Data to Improve Schools

Examples of Modules and Questions from the School Staff Survey (California School Climate Survey—CSCS)

Topics	Sample Questions
1. School Social and Academic Climate	This school is a supportive and inviting place for students to learn; is a supportive and inviting place for staff to work.
2. Discipline and Safety	Handles discipline problems fairly; is a safe place for students
3. Adult Support of Students	How many adults really care about every student?
4. Adult Mutual Support	How many adults support and treat each other with respect?
5. Need for Professional Development	Areas such as: meeting academic standards; evidence-based methods of instruction; serving English language learners
6. Perceptions of Students	How many students are motivated to learn; are well behaved?
7. Problems in School	How much of a problem at this school is student alcohol and drug use?; racial/ethnic conflict among students?
8. School Policies and Practices	This school promotes personnel participation in decisionmaking that affects school practices and policies; provides complete state-adopted instructional materials for students with IEPs.
Military Module	
1. Military-Connected Students and Needs and Strengths	Many military students have additional educational needs; Military students have additional strengths due to their family circumstances.
2. School's Inclusion of Military-Connected Students	This school provides a welcoming environment to military students and their families; has additional services for students whose parents are deployed.
3. Need for Professional Development Related to Military-Connected Students	I need professional development in order to understand military culture; understand the effects of deployment cycles.

Topics	Sample Questions
Additional Sections/Modules	
Staff who have responsibilities for services or instruction related to health, prevention, discipline, counseling, and/or safety	This school collaborates well with community organizations to help address substance use or other problems among youth; punishes first-time violations of alcohol or other drug policies by at least an out-of-school suspension.
	To what extent the school provides nutritional instruction?; alcohol or drug use prevention instruction?
School personnel with responsibilities for teaching or providing related services to students with individualized education programs (IEPs).	This school integrates special education into its daily operations; has a climate that encourages me to continue in my role of service to students with IEPs.

Examples of Modules and Questions from the California School Parent Survey

Topics	Sample Questions
1. Background	Does one or more of your children receive a free or reduced-price breakfast or lunch at this school?; In what grade is your child?
2. Perceptions of School	Promotes academic success for *all* students; gives my child opportunities to participate in classroom activities
3. School Problems	Student alcohol and drug use?; weapons possession?
4. School Policies and Practices	Actively seeks the input of parents before making important decisions; has a supportive learning environment for my child
Military Module	
1. Background	How many times have you been deployed outside the United States?
2. Importance of School Factors	Academic reputation; convenience
3. Need for Additional Services	Additional tutoring; after-school activities
4. Satisfaction	The respect school staff show to military families?; The understanding teachers show you as a military parent?

6. Using Data to Improve Schools

OTHER STATES FOCUSING
ON MILITARY STUDENTS

California is not the only state that is beginning to use data to better support these families. For example, in Illinois, legislation was written that would ask schools to identify if they have military students so that counseling and other services could be provided when a parent is deployed.

The bill grew out of the efforts of the National Guard and Reserves to identify schools that enroll significant numbers of military children. The information would allow the National Guard to send military liaisons into schools to support children at times that could be more stressful.

Other states and districts also have school climate surveys and health risk and behavior surveys that could be modified or supplemented to better capture the concerns and experiences of military students.

BUILDING TRUST AND MOTIVATION

Once you know which survey instrument will be administered in your school, it's important to make the experience positive and productive. In this age of No Child Left Behind and other accountability efforts, many teachers, parents—and even administrators—have grown skeptical and even cynical toward anything that has to do with data collection or research. Why is the data being collected? How will it be used? And will it reflect badly on our school, teachers, and students? In addition, outside researchers often gain access to schools, conduct studies and interviews, and then generate reports that are either never available or are not relevant to students, parents, and staff. Given this climate of disillusionment, it is necessary to first build trust with members of the school community and to explain how participating in the effort can be a democratic and empowering process.

One way to gradually build this trust is to take small steps—such as focus groups on a specific topic with teachers, parents, and students—and to provide feedback to those participants and perhaps to the whole school as soon as possible. Describe what was learned by the process and what the school is going to do in response to the input. For example, schools across the country are all working to make their lunch programs healthier while also serving food that students will eat. Many schools have recruited students for tasting sessions so officials can see what menu creations students respond well to and which ones they refuse to try. The students are involved in choosing what will be served in their schools before it is prepared for everyone.

INCLUDING MULTIPLE PERSPECTIVES

It's also important to involve all members of the school community in your information-gathering efforts—students, parents, other community members, and staff. Also, don't only include teachers. Paraprofessionals, secretaries, custodians, after-school providers, and other staff members may be able to provide a valuable perspective that you might otherwise miss. Asking for their input also conveys the message that everyone in the school plays a role in helping children be healthy and successful. Likewise, members of the community—particularly those connected to the military—may be able to provide insight into problems or behavior that students might be showing outside of school.

Qualitative methods, such as mapping and focus groups, can be used to gather a variety of perspectives and can result in specific solutions to problems that have been identified.

FLEXIBILITY IS KEY

Not every school, and not every district, however, is interested in the same information. That's why it's important to have surveys that can be customized to include questions of interest to your school community, in addition to having standard sections so that results can be compared across schools within a district, or across districts within a state.

A framework for deciding which questions to ask—and how to ask them—can be helpful for creating survey instruments that meet your school's needs.

1. **Descriptive**: The purpose of these questions is to gather basic facts about issues that are relevant to the climate for students in your school. These might include questions like:

    - How many students feel that the school is safe?
    - How often did students see a weapon in school?
    - To what extent do students feel supported by staff in your school?
    - What is the proportion of students who are drinking alcohol on school grounds?
    - How proud are students of their school?

    These questions help you see where you stand and the current characteristics of your school in the areas such as safety, drug use, social climate, or mental health needs.

    Answers to these types of questions will typically include phrases such as "60% of our students report that they feel there is at least one adult at school who cares about them" or "half of our parents believe we are doing a good job preventing bullying."

2. **Comparisons between groups within your school**: You might also want to know how the answers to the descriptive questions vary for groups within your school community. For example, are military students more likely to say they are being bullied? Is alcohol use more prevalent among a certain demographic group or grade level in the school? Are there differences in responses between military students with a deployed parent and those whose parents are not deployed?

These questions help provide more detailed information and help you pinpoint sub-groups that may require different responses and special attention. For example, instead of just asking how many students were involved in cyber-bullying, you might find that girls are more likely than boys to engage in this behavior, pointing to the conclusion that education and prevention on this topic should be increased for girls.

It's typical to compare students by gender or ethnic group, but it can also be helpful to use other comparisons. You may ask questions about differences between students that are doing well academically and others, and between students who are involved in sports or other social activities and students who are less socially involved.

Another useful comparison is between groups that received specialized interventions or participated in certain school programs and those who did not. Such a comparison will help you see whether the participation in a program or intervention is associated with any positive gains. For instance, do students who engaged in a year-long program to improve socio-emotional learning respond differently than other students? It's also important to consider differences between groups of parents. Are working parents having more trouble attending school events than nonworking parents? Do parents of girls worry more about "sexting" than parents of boys? Answers to these questions can help your school implement solutions or provide workshops that address parents' concerns.

Staff members should also not be seen as one homogeneous group. Do their responses vary based on the grade or subject they teach, the position they hold in the school, their years of experience, their race, ethnicity, or gender?

3. **Comparisons between schools or districts**: These comparisons are useful for identifying and addressing areas of concern on a broader level and for putting your own results in perspective. For example, you may learn that less than 10% of your students considered bringing a weapon to school. Of course, you don't want to hear that *any* students are considering bringing weapons to school. But how does that compare to what students are saying at other schools in the district, or in

other districts across the state? If the figures are higher than 10% at other schools in your district, you may still decide to try and change the situation in your school. But this is quite different than learning that the figures in most other schools are closer to 2%. Such comparisons help to put your figures in perspective.

4. **Change over time**: If this is a survey that is given annually, or every few years, you can also look at whether change has occurred over time and whether different groups within your school have experienced more or less change over time. If your school serves a large proportion of military children, or has high turnover among students in general, you may not be able to capture responses from the same group of students, but you can determine some information about certain trends within your school, or whether your policies and practices are having any effect on areas you are trying to address.

For example, do more or fewer students today report experimenting with marijuana or other drugs than the last time the question was asked? Do military students report feeling more or less welcome in the school compared with 2 years ago? Do parents or students feel that discipline policies are more or less fair than on the previous survey? If change has occurred in your school in the areas covered by the questions, how does it compare to changes that have taken place at other schools or districts? Did you see more or less success from district-wide initiatives or interventions?

USING THE DATA

Ultimately you want these school climate and risk and resiliency surveys to help you identify the strengths and weaknesses among military and other students in your school and to guide your staff in setting goals for the coming year. These results can be used to complete school improvement plans, apply for grant funding, or even respond to policymakers if survey results are made public.

If your district, for example, is implementing Positive Behavioral Interventions and Support (PBIS)—or another initiative or grant-funded program—but can only afford to include a certain number of schools in the training, both quantitative and qualitative information can be used to identify whether your school should be involved. These surveys can also assist your school in implementing Response to Intervention (RTI), a method designed to better identify which students are having trouble learning and might qualify for special education. Military students may sometimes be placed in special education when it's possible that issues related to being in a military family were contributing to their learning difficulties.

6. Using Data to Improve Schools

Additional steps are needed, however, to translate those results into policies and practices that contribute to student success and reinforce the sense among students and others that it was worthwhile to participate in the process.

MAPPING

Mapping is a technique that can be used to identify locations within a school where problem behavior might be more likely to occur. This could include violence or threats of violence among students, theft, bullying, or drug and alcohol use on school property.

Your school's use of mapping could focus on just one of those problems. Mapping doesn't require extensive training and is a valuable tool because it can include all stakeholders–students, teachers, and other staff members–in providing their perspectives on where such "hot spots" are located in the school, at what times of day the behavior occurs, and who is present when it happens. An important part of the process is gathering each person's thinking on why specific times and locations within the school are more prone to these situations.

- **Get a map**. The map ideally will include all common areas, classrooms, restrooms, offices, and other spaces within the school as well as outside areas, including the playground, and even the routes students might take if they are walking to and from school.
- **Make two copies for each person**. Each person participating in the mapping process should receive two identical copies of the map. One map should be used by each participant to determine where they have experienced, seen, or have personal knowledge of problem behaviors that are taking place. On the map, they should highlight up to three of the worst cases of the behavior. Next to each of those they should also provide:
  1. the general time frame that it took place (before school, after school, between classes, during a schoolwide event or game)
  2. the grade and gender of the students involved in the incident
  3. their own knowledge of whether the incident was reported to an adult at the school and how school officials responded (e.g., whether students were sent to the principal's office, suspended, sent to peer counseling, etc.)

This kind of descriptive information should be shared during a group discussion.

On the second map, participants should circle areas inside or outside the school that they consider to be their favorite areas of the

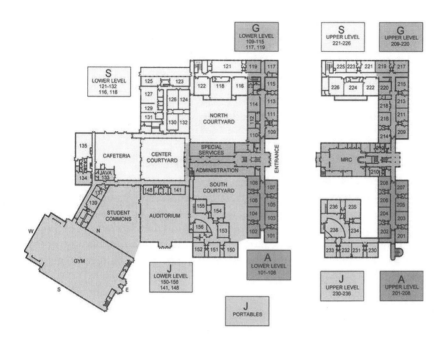

school–those where they feel safe or enjoy hanging out with their friends. This can provide an understanding of why certain places at certain times are more positive than others, perhaps leading to adjustments being made in other locations or at other times.

- **Ask for solutions**. The facilitator leading the discussions should also explore participants' ideas for solutions to the specific problems and ask what obstacles they may see to implementing a solution. Recognize that students, teachers, and administrators may all have different views on how the school should respond to these patterns. Ongoing discussions can generate workable solutions to the problem.

Schools that have used the mapping process to address issues of violence or bullying in their schools have found it to be effective. For example, one high school learned that fights or other violent events were occurring among 11th and 12th graders right outside a gym next to the parking lot immediately after school. Students and teachers agreed that the visible presence of school staff should be increased in and around the parking lot for 20 minutes after school.

In another school, students repeatedly reported during the mapping process that they felt unsafe near the school gate at the end of day. The information was relayed to the principal, who then observed the flow of traffic

6. Using Data to Improve Schools

through the gate, making sure she was not noticed by the students. After a couple of observations, she concluded that since only one gate was open, the clustering of students trying to exit the gate all at one time led to pushing, shoving, and skirmishes among impatient students. As a solution, she simply opened up another gate to ease the congestion. She further decided to assign teachers to greet the students as they were leaving school, making sure to call students by their names and express an interest in how their day went.

STUDENT LISTENING CIRCLE

Another method that has been found to give adults incredible insight into what students are thinking and feeling is known as the "fishbowl" technique. It has been used as a way to help schools understand data from the CHKS on student resiliency and youth development. In schools that use this approach, the adults have remained committed to implementing the changes suggested as a result of the process.

The listening circle is a special type of focus group that includes eight to ten students who respond to five or six questions based on data from the survey on nonacademic barriers to learning. Roughly the same number of adults is chosen to listen to what the students have to say. Three simultaneous listening circles are often held as part of a forum. One focuses on the role of the family, another on the role of the school, and the third on the community.

Typical questions asked during the listening circles include:

- How do you know when adults in your school care about you? What do they say and do?
- How do you know when an adult believes in you? What do they say and do?
- What would make school/learning more fun and interesting for you and your friends? What would you like to do?
- What kinds of decisions have you made and would you like to make in your classrooms and about your school?
- What kinds of things do you or could you do at school that would make a difference? That would help others? That would improve your school?
- Is there anything else you need from the adults in your school to help you achieve your goals and dreams?

Source: WestEd

WestEd's publication, "Guide to a School-Family-Community-School Partnership: Using a Student & Data Driven Process to Improve School Climates & Promote Student Success," provides details on the steps involved in planning and implementing the listening circle and forum process. Here is an overview:

Planning the Forum

- Identify a "resilience support coordinator," someone who plans the forum, is familiar with the data, and has positive relationships with students, teachers, and parents. This person also has a strong belief in listening to and learning from students' voices.
- Gather and examine the data.
- Recruit participants. Use short classroom presentations to explain the purpose of the focus group and offer incentives to attract interest. Choose a gender-balanced group of students from different grades and ethnic groups. Don't just choose students who frequently participate in school events and activities. Use similar guidelines in selecting adult participants from among staff, parents, and community members. Follow up frequently prior to the event.
- Obtain parental permission for students to be involved, photographed, or quoted.
- Select experienced facilitators for the focus groups who will ask the questions and guide students in turning complaints about their

schools or teachers into positive suggestions. Some schools have found it helpful to have an outsider as a facilitator.

- Schedule roughly four to five hours for the entire forum, which includes introductions, preparing both students and adults for the listening circle, breaks, the actual focus groups, time to eat, reporting on what was said, and time for discussions and recommendations. The circles also need a note taker, a time keeper, and materials such as chart paper, markers, and tape.

Conducting the Forum

- Prepare students for the day. Students will go directly to their break-out, listening circle rooms, while adults remain together to receive an overview of resilience, the data being focused on, and their role in listening respectfully to the students. Students receive training on speaking out and are told that the listening circle questions are intended to make them feel more positive about and connected with their schools.
- For the listening circle, students sit in a tight circle, while the adults sit in another circle outside the students. This way, the students look at each other and not the adults who are listening.
- Questions are asked one at a time and each student is given a chance to answer. Two people—one adult and one student—volunteer to serve as note takers and later report back to the group on what was said.
- Students are given color-coded note cards—a different color for each question—and are asked to write down three answers for each question. This way they will still have something to say if another student uses their answer. Ask students to give specific suggestions and examples.
- The students and adults then form one large circle and an initial discussion begins.
- The student-adult team reports back to the entire group on what the students had to say. Common themes across the listening circles are identified, solutions are suggested, and specific steps are scheduled.

In the schools that have used this strategy, tangible improvements have been made based on the feedback provided by the students. For example, in one school, students complained that they often had tests in more than one subject on the same day. In response, a more manageable schedule was created to avoid those situations. In another school, students complained about the condition of the restrooms. So administrators made sure they were promptly cleaned and regularly stocked with toilet paper, paper towels, and soap. In a third school, a mentoring program was created involving not only teachers, but also other school staff members.

CONCLUSION

Online and paper surveys, and more interactive methods, such as mapping and focus groups, are all ways to both collect information and communicate back with those who have a stake in the results. Including military students and parents in the process can reveal perceptions about your school that you might not have considered, and show these families that they are valued as part of the school community.

CHAPTER 7

Evidence-Based and Evidence-Informed Programs

School leaders are now extremely aware that if they are going to adopt a program or intervention in their school, there had better be some evidence that it is effective. Many grant-making organizations now require that schools select only interventions and programs that are designated as "evidence-based." The chances are also good that your school is already using evidence-based practices that address a variety of issues–whether it's a reading program, an anti-bullying program, or an effort to encourage positive behavior.

It's important to realize, however, that most–if not all–of the interventions that are now considered to be based on evidence were not designed with military children in mind. Experimental trials or pilot programs most likely never took into account the unique challenges that children in military families are facing.

For example, your school may have a bullying prevention program that teaches children to accept others who are different because of what they wear, whether they have a disability, or are gay. But military children may be subjected to teasing just because they have a parent who is in the military or because they have moved six or seven times and haven't had the same experiences as their peers.

For a military child, engaging in risky behavior, whether it is sexual activity or using drugs and alcohol, may increase when his or her parent has left for a deployment or after a parent has returned from war and is having trouble readjusting to family life.

Understand that your teachers, social workers, and counselors will likely have to adapt programs and practices to address the needs of the military students in your school. An anti-bullying program can include information on military culture, for example. A tutoring or mentoring program can reach out to veterans to work with military students who are struggling academically. College access programs should include information on military scholarships and rules regarding in-state tuition eligibility.

This is another reason why it's important to know how many children in your school have parents in the military. Then your surveys—whether they focus on risk and resiliency factors among students or parent attitudes toward the school—will be more meaningful and will more accurately reflect the needs in your population.

FINDING EVIDENCE-BASED PROGRAMS

Because there are not many evidence-based programs for military children, we have listed more general sources that are available to school leaders searching for effective programs. These institutes and agencies have examined the research on various programs and interventions and present it in a searchable format.

- The Center for the Study and Prevention of Violence at the University of Colorado has an Information Clearinghouse as well as a "Blueprints for Violence Prevention" project that identifies "truly outstanding violence and drug prevention programs that meet a high scientific standard of effectiveness." Blueprints features both model and promising programs. The selection criteria are also explained. http://www.colorado.edu/cspv/infohouse/index.html
- The Substance Abuse and Mental Health Services Administration (SAMHSA) is part of the U.S. Department of Health and Human Services. Its National Registry of Evidence-Based Programs and Practices (NREPP) includes hundreds of prevention and intervention programs that have been reviewed and rated by outside researchers. Ratings are explained, but they don't necessarily imply endorsement by SAMHSA. http://www.nrepp. samhsa.gov/Search.aspx
- What Works Clearinghouse is a database from the Institute of Educational Sciences within the U.S. Department of Education. Programs, practices, and policies are organized into the categories of Academic Achievement, Dropout Prevention, Language Development, Math/Science, Personal/Social Development, and Reading/Writing. http://ies.ed.gov/ncee/wwc/ A newer, related site is "Doing What Works," which focuses more on implementing best practices. http://dww.ed.gov/
- The Office of Juvenile Justice and Delinquency Prevention, part of the U.S. Department of Justice, offers a Model Programs Guide designed to assist educators and other youth-serving organizations in finding programs that can make a positive difference. The database includes over 200 programs. http://www.ojjdp.gov/mpg/

7. Evidence-Based Programs

- The Child Welfare Information Gateway is part of the U.S. Department of Health and Human Services' Administration for Children and Families. The Gateway lists evidence-based and evidence-informed programs in the area of parent education. http://www.childwelfare.gov/pubs/issue_briefs/parented/programs.cfm
- The "What Works" section of the Child Trends website features the Lifecourse Interventions to Nurture Kids Successfully (LINKS) Database, which includes programs that work—or don't—to enhance children's development. Also in the "What Works" section is a link to "Interventions that Work." http://www.childtrends.org/_catdisp_page.cfm?LID=CD56B3D7-2F05-4F8E-BCC99B05A4CAEA04
- A staff at the RAND Corporation maintains the Promising Practices Network. "Programs that Work" are organized into two categories: Proven and Promising Programs, which have met certain evidence criteria, and Screened Programs, which have not yet received a full review by the network. http://www.promisingpractices.net/default.asp

In Appendix B, we list many of these interventions, websites for more information, and some findings on their effectiveness. Again, while we have tried to provide the most up-to-date website address, you should conduct your own Internet search for the program if the link is incorrect.

PROMISING INTERVENTIONS FOR MILITARY CHILDREN

There is still a lack of research-based programs designed specifically for military children attending public schools. One initiative, however, is aimed at helping families cope with the challenges of deployment and reintegration.

FOCUS, which stands for Families OverComing Under Stress, is based at the University of California, Los Angeles. It is a resiliency-training program for military children and families. In group settings, participants learn practical skills to cope with the challenges of deployment and reintegration when the deployed family member comes back home. More specifically, the program teaches:

- emotional regulation
- communication
- problem solving
- goal setting
- managing deployment reminders

FOCUS has also been adapted to serve families with young children, in response to research showing that even infants and toddlers can experience stress and depression. FOCUS for Early Childhood emphasizes the parent-child relationship. The family sessions are used to model and practice learned skills. The three main components of FOCUS for early childhood are psycho-education, creating a family narrative/time line, and skills training in the areas of emotional regulation, communication, problem solving, and goal setting.

In addition, FOCUS-Combat Injury is currently being researched as part of a randomized control study among U.S. Army soldiers and their families. The FOCUS-CI study will evaluate the impact of this adapted version of FOCUS for families of combat injured soldiers receiving care in both medical and home settings. The study is taking place at Walter Reed Army Hospital, Brooke Army Medical Center, and Madigan Army Medical Center, and is being funded by Congressional Directed Medical Research Programs.

The original FOCUS program is available at many installations across the country and in Japan. In addition, an online version is available. More information can be found at http://www.focusproject.org/.

Two additional programs that can be implemented by teachers in your school were not specifically designed for military children, but have been recommended for use with military children struggling with stress, behavior problems, or other issues that could surface as a result of being part of a military family.

Child Adult Relationship Enhancement (CARE) is an "evidence-informed" intervention that is an adaptation of Parent-Child Interaction Therapy (PCIT). This means that CARE is guided or inspired by findings from research but it has not yet been evaluated for its effectiveness. PCIT is designed for children ages 2 to 12 with behavior problems and a history of traumatic stress, as well as their parents, caregivers, and teachers. The program has been shown to improve caregivers' ability to manage problem behavior, reduce conflict, and increase positive interaction with the child.

CARE focuses on the three skills of Praise, Paraphrase, and Point-out-Behavior to connect children with the caregivers. Parents or caregivers learn to give positive commands and to use "selective ignoring" techniques to encourage better behavior.

CARE training can be useful to those working with children in a wide variety of settings, including child-care centers and schools.

Research on CARE is not yet available, but a body of evidence exists for PCIT. More information on CARE training is available from the Trauma Treatment Training Center at Cincinnati Children's Hospital. http://www.cincinnatichildrens.org/research/div/child-abuse/trauma-center/pcit.htm

7. Evidence-Based Programs

Support for Students Exposed to Trauma (SSET): This program was developed by researchers at RAND in collaboration with Marleen Wong, an Assistant Dean in the USC School of Social Work and a co-principal investigator for Building Capacity. It is based on a group intervention called Cognitive Behavioral Intervention for Trauma in Schools (CBITS), which is aimed at relieving symptoms of PTSD, depression, and general anxiety for children exposed to trauma, such as witnessing or being a victim of violence, being abused, or being in a disaster. The program was not originally intended for military children, but can apply to many of the situations they might be facing. Through drawing, talking, and completing outside assignments, children learn a variety of skills, such as how to relax, challenge negative or upsetting thoughts, solve social problems, and process traumatic memories and grief. The program includes ten sessions and typically targets children in grades 6–9, but has been used with children as young as 8.

In a randomized controlled study with children from Los Angeles Unified School District, children in the CBITS program had significantly greater improvement in PTSD and depressive symptoms compared to those on the wait list at a 3-month follow-up. Parents of children in the program also reported significantly improved child functioning compared with children in the wait-list group. The improvements were still seen at a subsequent follow-up at 6 months. Results from another study showed that those in the CBITS intervention group had significantly fewer self-reported symptoms of PTSD and depression than children in a comparison group.

While CBITS is meant to be led by a mental health professional, SSET can be used by teachers and even graduate students. The manual provides lesson plans, materials, and worksheets for use in a group setting. More information is available at http://www.rand.org/pubs/research_briefs/RB9443-1/index1.html.

The Building Capacity Project and Consortium

In addition to the publication of this resource guide, *Building Capacity to Create Highly Supportive Military-Connected School Districts* has several other components:

- Master's students in social work, school counseling, and school psychology, receiving special training in working with military-connected schools, are based in the consortium schools. They provide a range of services for the entire school community, but primarily focus on the needs of military students and their families. These services include individual and group consultations with students, staff, and parents, and the dissemination of resources and materials designed to increase knowledge within schools.
- Their role also includes parent support, data collection and interpretation, and after-school programs. Their work in the schools is designed to create a military-friendly school climate that can be sustained once the project ends. Schools will be matched with evidence-based programs appropriate for their student population as well as community-based and district-level resources that meet the needs of their families. Over the 4-year grant period, interns will provide an estimated 72,000 contact hours in schools and the community.
- Conducted since 1985, the *California Health Kids Survey* collects detailed information on school climate, risky behaviors, resiliency, and protective factors both in school and at home. The survey is administered by WestEd, an education research, development, and service agency. Because every school district in California is required to conduct the survey, it is a valuable tool for monitoring students' needs and behaviors. The Building Capacity project trains the interns, teachers, parent organizations, and principals to make better use of this data system in their decisions about programs and services for students.

- In addition, the state of California and WestEd have partnered with the consortium to administer a newly created *Military Module* of the survey, which is now available to all schools in the state and nation. This module is allowing schools to examine how deployment and multiple school changes, as well as school, home, and community supports, impact students' social and academic outcomes.
- Building Capacity is also identifying innovative and successful practices within schools that create more supportive environments for military families. These programs and best practices are being evaluated to determine whether they can be replicated in other schools. These ideas will be collected and housed at USC as part of a clearinghouse. In addition, since there are currently no existing evidence-based models designed specifically for military-connected schools, this project will adapt existing programs for use with these students and families and evaluate their effectiveness.
- To build awareness and encourage the exchange of ideas surrounding military-connected schools, Building Capacity is arranging conferences and workshops for administrators and educators in the consortium schools. This aspect of the project builds on the work already started by DoDEA, military school liaison officers, and nonprofit organizations such as the Military Child Education Coalition. In addition, these gatherings will be adapted to address the individual needs of schools.
- Finally, it is our hope that the schools and districts participating in this project will continue this work once the grant expires. Another goal of Building Capacity is that the work implemented in the San Diego-area districts can be replicated in military-connected schools across the country.

The school districts involved in the project are located in San Diego and Riverside counties in California. San Diego County is home to Camp Pendleton Marine Corps Base, Naval Base Coronado, Marine Corps Air Station Miramar, Naval Base Point Loma, and the Space and Naval Warfare Systems Command's Systems Center Pacific.

The eight school districts in the consortium are:

- **Bonsall Union School District**: Located north of San Diego, this is the smallest district in the consortium with 1,881 students. Approximately 9% of the elementary district's students are from military families. The district is 52% White, 34% Hispanic, 6% Asian, and 2% African American.
- **Chula Vista Elementary School District**: Located south of San Diego near the border with Mexico, the 27,460-student district

serves 2,600 military students—9.5% of its enrollment. The district is over 65% Hispanic, 12% White, almost 13% Asian, and 4% African American.

- **Escondido Union Elementary School District**: Northeast of San Diego, this 19,300-student district serves 1,931 students from military families—10% of its enrollment. The district is 65% Hispanic, 25% White, 5% Asian, and 3% African American.
- **Escondido Union High School District**: 9% of the enrollment in this 9,350-student district is from military families. This district is 55% Hispanic, 35% White, 5% Asian, and 3% African American.
- **Fallbrook Union Elementary School District**: With two schools located on the Camp Pendleton base, this elementary district serves 1,500 military students—over 27% of its 5,600-student enrollment. This district is 49% Hispanic, 39% White, 5% African American, and 3% Asian.
- **Fallbrook Union High School District**: Located in North San Diego County, this 3,100-student district serves 313 military students—10% of its enrollment. The district is 47% Hispanic, 41% White, 3% Asian, and 2% African American.
- **Oceanside Unified School District**: Located north of San Diego, this 21,500-student district serves the second largest percentage of military students—about 19%, or 3,858 students. The K–12 district is 53% Hispanic, 29% White, 8% Asian, and 8% African American.
- **Temecula Valley Unified School District**: Northeast of San Diego, this K–12 district is the largest in the consortium with 28,780 students—2%, or 579 of which are from military families. This district is 50% White, 20% Hispanic, 10% Asian, and 4% African-American. 14% of students are identified as multiracial or gave no response.

Evidence-Based Programs That Could Be Adapted for Military-Connected Schools

Midwestern Prevention Project (now called Project STAR)

http://www.colorado.edu/cspv/blueprints/modelprograms/MPP.html
http://www.childtrends.org/Lifecourse/programs/MidwesternPreventionProject.
   htm

- *Goals:* To help youth see the tremendous social pressure to use drugs and find ways for them to avoid their use and those situations through the help of school, parents, the community, and the media.
- *Target Outcomes:* The reduction of adolescent drug use and the involvement of parents and community. [In this Appendix, "Goals" are the overall goals of the program, while the "Target Outcomes" are what is being measured by an evaluation or study.]
- *Populations:* From early adolescence through middle and late adolescence. Programs begin in 6th and 7th grade.
  - ➢ 1,000 middle school students
  - ➢ 20 teachers
  - ➢ 12 parents
  - ➢ 3–4 principals
  - ➢ 4 student leaders
- *Problem:* Adolescent drug use and community involvement.
- *Intervention:*
  - ➢ Mass media programs
  - ➢ School program and frequent boosters
    - ✓ Role playing models in class
    - ✓ Discussion groups with student and teachers
    - ✓ Homework assignments to involve parents
  - ➢ Parent educational organization
    - ✓ Parent-principal committee
  - ➢ Community organization and training sessions

- ➤ Local policy changes:
  - ✓ Alcohol
  - ✓ Drugs
  - ✓ Tobacco
- ➤ Parent-principal committee that meets to review policy and parent-child communication training
- ➤ All programs deliver a constant anti-drug message via all of the components
- *Resources needed:*
  - ➤ $175,000 minimum over a 3-year period
    - ✓ Costs of teacher, parent, and community leader training
    - ✓ Curriculum materials for school-based program
    - ✓ $4,000 for each group trained
    - ✓ $100–125 for each trainer manual
    - ✓ $7 for each student workbook
- *Results:*
  - ➤ 40% reduction in daily smoking
  - ➤ Similar reductions in marijuana use and alcohol use through grade 12
  - ➤ Prevention shown through age 23
  - ➤ Increased parent-child communication
  - ➤ The program also led to more development of prevention programs, activities, and services among the community
- *Assessment:* Regular meetings to assess programs and to improve them

Big Brothers Big Sisters of America

http://www.colorado.edu/cspv/blueprints/modelprograms/BBBS.html
http://www.bbbs.org/site/c.diJKKYPLJvH/b.1539751/k.BDB6/Home.htm

- *Goals:* To provide adult support and friendship to youth in one-to-one relationships.
- *Target Outcomes:* To build relationships between youths from single-parent homes and adult volunteers.
- *Populations:* Youths from age 6–18 from single-parent homes. Also involves adult volunteers and parental involvement for meetings and updates.
- *Problem:* This program is designed to address the problem of youth violence and drug abuse in the hopes that a one-on-one relationship with an adult will deter youths from engaging in these behaviors.
- *Intervention:* The program has several procedures that all involved in the program must go through.
  - ➤ An orientation with the program is required for all the volunteers.
  - ➤ Volunteers must be screened by an application, background check, and an assessment of whether they will be able to honor their time commitments.
  - ➤ The youth in the program are assessed by a written application, interviews with them and their parents, and assessment of their home life. This is to help

make the best match between child and volunteer and to involve the parents
and obtain their permission.

➤ The matches are made according to the needs of the child, the abilities of the
volunteer, and program and preferences of the parent.

➤ Contact between parent, volunteer, and child is made within 2 weeks of match,
then monthly telephone contact with the parent/child and volunteer throughout
the first year and quarterly contact with all during the entire match.

➤ Program can last from age 6 to age 18, starting at any age in between. It lasts
as long as everyone is committed and involved.

• *Results:* These numbers are in comparison to youths who did not participate in
the program.

➤ 46% less likely to initiate drug use during the study period

➤ 27% less likely to initiate alcohol use

➤ 33% less likely to hit someone

➤ Improvement in academic behavior, attitudes, and performance

➤ More likely to have higher quality relationships with their parents or
guardians

➤ More likely to have higher quality relationships with their peers at the end of
the study

✓ These figures were the result of a study done in 1992 and 1993 with
1,000 10–16-year-olds from eight agencies around the country. Half were
matched with volunteers and the other half were put on a program waitlist.
The activities of the two groups were then monitored for 18 months and
compared to one another.

Functional Family Therapy

http://www.colorado.edu/cspv/blueprints/modelprograms/FFT.html
http://www.ncjrs.gov/pdffiles1/ojjdp/184743.pdf

• *Goals:* Targets kids who have demonstrated a range of maladaptive and
behavioral problems.

• *Target Outcomes:* To prevent and treat youth with these problematic behaviors and
provide a resource for their families and community.

• *Populations:* Youth aged 11–18 at risk for delinquency and other behavioral
problems. Also involves the parents and therapy teams.

• *Problem:* Youth violence, substance abuse, delinquency, oppositional defiant
disorder, or disruptive behavior disorder.

• *Intervention:*

➤ 8–12 hours of time

➤ 1–2-person teams in:

✓ house of participant

✓ clinic

✓ juvenile court

➤ *Presented by:*
   ✓ para-professionals under supervision
   ✓ trained probation officers
   ✓ mental health technicians
   ✓ degreed mental health professionals
➤ Program phases
   ✓ Engagement which is designed to prevent early program dropout
   ✓ Motivation which creates lasting emotional changes in the areas of beliefs, trust, hopes, and increased alliances
   ✓ Assessment of relationships between the individuals, families, and community members
   ✓ Behavior change which involves communications training, specific tasks, technical aids, basic parenting skills, contracting, and response-cost techniques
   ✓ Generalization in which family case management is guided by individualized family functional needs as to their environment, community, and resources
- *Resources:* 90-day costs for two ongoing programs are between $1,350 and $3,760 for an average of 12 home visits per family.
- *Results:*
   ➤ Effective treatment of adolescents with multiple mental problems
   ➤ Interrupting matriculation of these students into higher cost programs
   ➤ Preventing younger children from entering infrastructure of care
   ➤ Preventing young adults from entering adult criminal system
   ➤ Effectively transferring treatment effects across treatment systems

Life Skills Training

http://www.colorado.edu/cspv/blueprints/modelprograms/LST.html
http://www.lifeskillstraining.com/
http://nrepp.samhsa.gov/ViewIntervention.aspx?id=109

- *Goals:* Intervention in middle schools to combat early drug and alcohol use.
- *Target Outcomes:* A reduction in the number of younger students doing drugs and a reduction in the number who do drugs in the future.
- *Populations:* Middle school students in grades 6 and 7. Administered by teachers, health professionals, and peer leaders.
- *Problem:* Program addresses the problem of adolescent drug use by attacking this problem early.
- *Intervention:*
   ➤ General self-management skills
      ✓ Social skills on and skills relating to drug use
   ➤ Skill are taught by:
      ✓ instruction

- ✓ demonstration
- ✓ feedback
- ✓ reinforcement
- ✓ practice
  - ➢ Used in schools for 3 years
- *Resources:*
  - ➢ $7 a year per student for curriculum materials
  - ➢ $2,000 per day of training for 1 or 2 days
- *Results:*
  - ✓ Reduced tobacco use, marijuana, and alcohol by 50%–75%
  - ➢ Follow up after 6 years also showed that the program:
    - ✓ Reduced the use of multiple drugs by 66%
    - ✓ Reduced the smoking of one pack of cigarettes per day by 25%
    - ✓ Decreased use of inhalants, narcotics, and hallucinogens

Multisystemic Therapy (MST)

http://www.colorado.edu/cspv/blueprints/modelprograms/MST.html
http://www.mstservices.com/
http://nrepp.samhsa.gov/ViewIntervention.aspx?id=26

- *Goals:* To address the multiple factors in adolescents' lives that lead to serious antisocial behavior in juvenile offenders. This means not only working with the adolescents, but also working with their families and communities in order to address the larger problems that lead to this sort of behavior.
- *Target Outcomes:* To create behavioral changes in the juvenile offender and change their environment.
- *Populations:* Adolescents from 12–17 who are chronic, violent, or substance abusing juvenile offenders, who are also at a high risk of out-of-home placements. The program also involves parents, community members, case workers, and therapists.
- *Problem:* Serious adolescent behavioral problems, such as drug use, violence, and criminal activity.
- *Intervention:*
  - ➢ Home-based model of delivery
    - ✓ parents are given the skills to deal with their kids' issues at home
    - ✓ developmentally appropriate demands are put on child and family by case workers
    - ✓ family therapy and strategic planning with a therapist
    - ✓ 60 hours of therapy over a period of 4 months, or catered to the needs and availability of the family
- *Resources:* $4,500 per youth
- *Results:*
  - ➢ Reduction of 20–70% in rate of re-arrests

➢ Reduction of 47–64% in out-of-home placements
➢ Extensive improvement in family functioning
➢ Decreased mental health problems for serious juvenile offenders

Nurse Family Partnership

http://www.colorado.edu/cspv/blueprints/modelprograms/NFP.html
http://www.nursefamilypartnership.org/
http://nrepp.samhsa.gov/ViewIntervention.aspx?id=88

- *Goals:* To provide knowledge and help to pregnant mothers in order to create the best environment for them and their babies.
- *Target Outcomes:* To decrease violence, substance abuse, and arrests of both the mother and the child in the future.
- *Problem:* Low-income pregnant mothers are ill-prepared to deal with their pregnancy and the birth of their child and need to be educated and helped in order to be good mothers and raise productive and non-aggressive children.
- *Intervention:*
  ➢ A nurse visits the woman during pregnancy and afterward
    ✓ to improve outcome of pregnancy and prenatal health
    ✓ to improve care given to infants and toddlers
    ✓ to improve woman's developing career, education, and future pregnancies
    ✓ one nurse is assigned to a family for duration of visits
- *Resources:* Program costs $3,200 per year for the first few years of the program, later it will only cost $2,800 after the nurses and administrators have all been trained and the program begins to work smoothly. Funding can often be found in government programs for welfare reform, child abuse prevention, and other related areas.
- *Results:*
    ✓ 79% fewer reports of child abuse by women in program
    ✓ 31% fewer subsequent births
    ✓ An average of 2 years or more between birth of first and second child
    ✓ 30 months fewer government aid to families
    ✓ 44% fewer maternal behavior problems related to alcohol
    ✓ 69% fewer maternal arrests
  ➢ 15 years later the children of women in the program were found to have
    ✓ 56% fewer arrests of 15-year-olds and less alcohol consumption
    ✓ 60% fewer episodes of 15-year-olds running away

Multidimensional Treatment Foster Care (MTFC)

http://www.colorado.edu/cspv/blueprints/modelprograms/MTFC.html
http://www.mtfc.com/

- *Goals:* To provide a positive and supportive family environment for juvenile offenders as an alternative to incarceration and hospitalization. Also for youth to develop good relationships with their foster families and to begin better habits and behaviors.
- *Target Outcomes:* Better-adjusted youth who will not return to violence, crime, or substance abuse and who have better relationships with their families and peers.
- *Populations:* Teens with a history of chronic or severe criminal behavior who are at a high risk of incarceration. Families in the community who agree to take on youths, caseworkers, biological families of youths, and other officers connected to the youths.
- *Problem:* Juvenile offenders need a better way to be rehabilitated than going to prison. This program aims to create a more comprehensive and multifaceted program for these adolescents.
- *Intervention:*
  - ➢ Foster parents are trained to provide a therapeutic environment for teens
    - ✓ parents attend weekly meetings and receive daily phone calls for support
  - ➢ Teens' biological families receive counseling with teens
    - ✓ goal is for teens to return home to their biological families
  - ➢ Coordination
    - ✓ frequent contact is maintained between teens' case workers, families, teachers, parole officers, and other concerned adults
- *Resources:* $2,691 per month per youth for an average stay of 7 months
- *Results:*
  - ➢ Youths spent 60% fewer days incarcerated at 12-month follow up
  - ➢ Fewer subsequent arrests
  - ➢ Running away from program reduced by two-thirds
  - ➢ Less hard drug use in follow-up period
  - ➢ Quicker community placement from more restrictive places like hospitals or detention centers

Olweus Bullying Prevention Program

http://www.colorado.edu/cspv/blueprints/modelprograms/BPP.html
http://www.clemson.edu/olweus/

- *Goals:* To reduce and prevent bullying in schools.
- *Target Outcomes:* Better school environments in which there are very few instances of bullying.
- *Populations:* Students in elementary, middle, and junior high schools, all students participate in the program, but students who are identified as bullies and victims of bullies participate in additional parts of the program.
- *Problem:* Bullying and victimization in schools.
- *Intervention:*
  - ➢ Schoolwide components

        ✓ anonymous questionnaire assesses the nature and prevalence of bullying
        ✓ conference to discuss the problem and possible interventions in the school
        ✓ formation of a bullying prevention coordinating committee
        ✓ increased supervision of students at bullying "hot spots"
    ➤ Classroom components
        ✓ rules against bullying and regular class meetings to discuss bullying and student behavior
    ➤ Individual component
        ✓ intervention with students identified as bullies or victims
        ✓ discussions with involved parents

- *Resources:*
  - ➤ Compensation for an onsite coordinator
  - ➤ Approximately $200 per school for questionnaire and computer programs
  - ➤ $65 per teacher to cover classroom materials
  - ➤ Program expenses vary depending on size and number of participating students
- *Results:*
  - ➤ Substantial reductions in both girls and boys reporting bullying
  - ➤ Substantial reduction in students' reports of antisocial behavior, vandalism, fighting, theft, and truancy
  - ➤ Substantial improvements in student reports of classroom atmosphere: more positive classroom relationships, more discipline, and more positive attitudes toward school and homework

Promoting Alternative Thinking Strategies (PATHS)

http://www.colorado.edu/cspv/blueprints/modelprograms/PATHS.html
http://nrepp.samhsa.gov/ViewIntervention.aspx?id=20

- *Goals:* To promote emotional and social competencies and reduce aggressive behavior in students.
- *Target Outcomes:* For children to be able to react in productive and competent ways to changes, schoolwork, social situations, and behavioral issues.
- *Populations:* All elementary age students in regular or special needs classrooms should be initiated upon starting school and program should be continued through 5th grade.
- *Problem:* Childhood aggression and behavioral problems and a lack of knowledge of how to deal with these issues.
- *Intervention:*
  - ➤ Program taught three times a week
    - ✓ provides teachers with curriculum for the prevention of violence and the promotion of self-control and positive peer relations among students
    - ✓ lessons include learning about and identifying feelings
    - ✓ teachers receive 2–3 days of training and have weekly meetings with the program coordinator

- *Resources:*
  - ➤ $15–$45 per student per year
  - ➤ High cost involves an onsite coordinator, and lower involves using current staff
- *Results:*
  - ➤ Improved self-control
  - ➤ Improved understanding and recognition of emotions
  - ➤ Increased ability to tolerate frustration
  - ➤ Use of effective conflict resolution strategies
  - ➤ Increased thinking and planning skills
  - ➤ Decreased anxiety and depression symptoms, behavioral problems
  - ➤ Decreased sadness, depression, and aggression

Incredible Years Series (IYS)

http://www.colorado.edu/cspv/blueprints/modelprograms/IYS.html
http://www.incredibleyears.com/
http://nrepp.samhsa.gov/ViewIntervention.aspx?id=93

- *Goals:* To treat emotional behavior and problems in young children through their parents and teachers and promote emotional competence.
- *Target Outcomes:* Reduction in childhood aggression and the development of skills to deal with emotional and peer-related problems in constructive ways.
- *Populations:* Children ages 2–8 who exhibit behaviors of aggression, defiance, and violence. Program involves the children's parents and teachers.
- *Problem:* Childhood behavioral problems with parents, teachers, and other children.
- *Intervention:*
  - ➤ Training for parents: Programs are to promote children's social competence and prevent behavioral problems through games, praise, incentives, limits, and ways to deal with misbehavior. Other programs deal with effective ways to communicate with one another, anger management, and problem solving. Another program focuses on helping children with school and homework, and developing positive outlooks for both.
  - ➤ Training for teachers: These programs focus on classroom management skills, such as distributing teacher attention, dealing with discipline problems, using praise and incentives, building relationships with students, and creating problem solving methods with students.
  - ➤ Training for children: These programs teach children ways of dealing with emotion, how to be friends, how to see from other' points of view, anger management skills, problem solving skills, school rules, and how to be a good student. These are created for small groups of students who show signs of behavioral problems.
- *Resources:*

- ➢ The Parent Training Programs cost $1,300 for the Basic program, $775 for the Advance program, and $995 for the School program.
- ➢ The Teacher Training Program costs $1,250.
- ➢ The Child Training Program costs $975.
- *Results:*
  - ➢ For six randomized control groups of parents:
    - ✓ Parents used more positive commands and praise and reduced the number of negative commands and comments.
    - ✓ Parents used more effective limit setting rules than harsh discipline and monitored children more effectively.
    - ✓ Parental confidence and family communication and problem solving increased while parental depression decreased.
    - ✓ Reduced behavioral problems for children while interacting with parents and better compliance with parents' commands.
  - ➢ For two randomized control groups of teachers:
    - ✓ Increased use of praise and positive encouragement and reduced use of punishment and criticism.
    - ✓ Increased cooperation of students with teachers, positive interaction with peers, and more positive views of and engagement with school and studies.
    - ✓ Reduction in conflict and aggression among students in the classroom.
  - ➢ For two randomized child training groups:
    - ✓ Increase in children's problem solving abilities and better conflict management skills with other students.
    - ✓ Reductions in conduct problems in the classroom and at home.

Project Towards No Drug Abuse (Project TND)

http://www.colorado.edu/cspv/blueprints/modelprograms/TND.html
http://www.promoteprevent.org/publications/ebi-factsheets/
    project-towards-no-drug-abuse-project-tnd
http://tnd.usc.edu/

- *Goals:* To prevent and reduce drug abuse in adolescents.
- *Target Outcomes:* Lower use of hard drugs, marijuana, alcohol, and cigarettes in 14–19-year-olds.
- *Populations:* 14–19-year-olds in all types of high schools using the regular program and experimental ones.
- *Problem:* Adolescent drug use and victimization.
- *Intervention:*
  - ➢ There are 12 in-class interactive sessions which cover a variety of topics that involve the use of drugs and alcohol:
    - ✓ Active listening
    - ✓ Stereotyping
    - ✓ Myths and denials

- ✓ Chemical dependency
- ✓ "Talk Show"
- ✓ Marijuana panel
- ✓ Tobacco use cessation
- ✓ Stress, health, and goals
- ✓ Self-control
- ✓ Positive and negative thought and behavior loops
- ✓ Perspectives
- ✓ Decisionmaking and commitment
- ➤ Each lesson lasts approximately 40–50 minutes and is for use over a 4-week period.
- ➤ The lessons involve information on the social and health implications of substance use and abuse, communication and stress management techniques, and self-control behaviors for older teens.
- *Resources:*
  - ➤ $70 per teacher's manual
  - ➤ $50 for 5 student workbooks
  - ➤ $2,500 for a 2-day training program and trainers' travel
- *Results:*
  - ➤ For 3,000 youths from 42 schools across three trials after the 1-year follow up:
    - ✓ 27% reduction in 30-day cigarette use
    - ✓ 22% reduction in 30-day marijuana use
    - ✓ 26% reduction in 30-day hard drug use
    - ✓ 9% reduction in 30-day drug use among baseline drinkers
    - ✓ 6% reduction in victimization by males

Across Ages

http://nrepp.samhsa.gov/ViewIntervention.aspx?id=138
http://acrossages.org/

- *Goals:* To give children the ability to develop positively and prevent them from engaging in behaviors like drug abuse, violence, or early sexual activity.
- *Target Outcomes:* Reduce children's use of substances and increase their social skills and parental involvement.
- *Populations:* Children ages 9–13 who live in communities with few positive free time activities and role models. They may be placed with outside families due to their own parents' inability to care for them.
- *Problem:* Drug abuse, poor social skills, and lack of parental and family involvement in the lives of children.
- *Intervention:*
  - ➤ Can be used as an in-school program or as an after-school program. In-school activities can take place in the classroom, after-school activities can take place in a school, community center, or a faith-based institution.

- ➤ Older adults (55+) must be involved as mentors. They must be recruited, trained, and spend a minimum of 2 hours a week in one-on-one contact with children.
- ➤ Youths must spend 1–2 hours a week performing community service.
- ➤ This program uses the Social Problem Solving module of the Social Competence Promotion Program for Young Adolescents which involves 26 weekly lessons of 45 minutes each on social competence training.
- ➤ Youth also engage in monthly weekend activities for them and their family members and mentors.
- ➤ Materials are available in Spanish and English.
- *Duration:* 1–3 years
  - ➤ 12 months of successful programming
  - ➤ Mentors spend a minimum of 2 hours per week with youths
  - ➤ Youth spend 1–2 hours per week doing community service
  - ➤ Twenty-six 45-minute lessons in Social Competence Training
  - ➤ Family activities once a month on a weekend
- *Resources:*
  - ➤ $1,000–$5,000
    - ✓ Training
    - ✓ Materials
- *Personnel:*
  - ➤ One full-time project director
  - ➤ One half-time project coordinator
  - ➤ One outreach coordinator
  - ➤ Support staff (each working 10 hours per week)
  - ➤ Mentors
- *Settings:* Rural, urban, or suburban
- *Results:*
  - ➤ Decrease in substance abuse
  - ➤ Increase in knowledge about and negative attitude toward drug use
  - ➤ Increased school attendance and improved grades, decreased suspensions
  - ➤ Improved attitudes of youths toward school and their future
  - ➤ Improved attitudes toward adults, especially older adults
  - ➤ Decrease in school absences

Al's Pals: Kids Making Healthy Choices

http://nrepp.samhsa.gov/ViewIntervention.aspx?id=116
http://www.wingspanworks.com/educational_programs/about_als_pals.php

- *Goals:* To help socialize young children so that they can express their feelings, relate to others, use self-control, resolve problems, make safe choices, and give them an environment in which they can practice these skills.
- *Target Outcomes:* Reduce future use of alcohol, drugs, reduce violent behavior,

antisocial behavior and increase emotional competence.

- *Populations:* Children ages 3–8 who exhibit early violent, antisocial, or sexual behavior.
- *Problem:* Childhood violence, early sexual activity, drug abuse, and antisocial behavior.
- *Intervention:*
  - ➤ 5–24 weeks for the program
  - ➤ Individual:
    - ✓ Life/social skills training
    - ✓ Classroom lessons to address addiction and substance abuse
    - ✓ Social group work in combination with social skills education
  - ➤ Family:
    - ✓ Parent education
  - ➤ Peer:
    - ✓ Classroom and peer activities created to develop expression, communication, positive peer relationships, and independent thinking
  - ➤ School:
    - ✓ Life skills training with student role playing
    - ✓ Changes in teaching approaches and parental involvement
  - ➤ In-/after-school classes:
    - ✓ Teacher delivers 10–15 minute lessons twice a week
    - ✓ Lessons include hand puppets Al and his friends Ty and Keisha and they involve the students in singing, role playing, and modeling positive social behaviors. Teachers then model and reinforce the skills throughout the day.
  - ➤ Booster session:
    - ✓ Nine follow-up lessons are used with 2nd- or 3rd-grade children who were previously involved in the program.
  - ➤ Parent training:
    - ✓ Sessions designed to teach parents how to express their feelings, listen to their children, become involved meaningfully, hold high expectations for their children, learn to solve problems, and enhance their parent-child relationship.
- *Resources:*
  - ➤ Classroom curriculum kit containing the tools for the 46 lessons
  - ➤ $1,000–$5,000 for the program training and materials
- *Settings:* Rural, urban, and suburban
- *Results:*
  - ➤ Significant decreases in negative behaviors in response to personal problems
  - ➤ Significant reduction in problem social behaviors
  - ➤ Participants are 2 to 5 times more likely to increase their use of positive classroom skills in response to problems
  - ➤ Participants are 1.5 to 4 times more likely to actually use their positive

response skills than children who did not participate
- *Reproduction:*
  - ➤ This program had multiple successful program implementations across the United States.

All Stars

http://nrepp.samhsa.gov/ViewIntervention.aspx?id=28
http://www.allstarsprevention.com/

- *Goals:* To prevent early adolescent use of drugs and alcohol and premature sexual activity, and to help students develop meaningful peer relationships and positive lifestyles and character.
- *Target Outcomes:* Reducing early adolescent drug use and negative behavior.
- *Populations:* 11–14 year olds.
- *Problem:* Risky early adolescent behavior that serves as gateway behavior for more and worse risky and negative behavior in the future.
- *Intervention:*
  - ➤ 1–3 year program
  - ➤ Students are involved in three formats which all involve:
    - ✓ Small group activities
    - ✓ Group discussions
    - ✓ Worksheet tasks
    - ✓ Video recording
    - ✓ Games
    - ✓ Art activities
  - ➤ Students also document their voluntary commitment to the program; sometimes they also receive symbolic reminders of their commitments.
  - ➤ Format 1: Teachers:
    - ✓ Thirteen 45-minute core classroom lessons
    - ✓ Eight 45-minute booster classroom lessons
    - ✓ Optional one-on-one meetings with students
    - ✓ Celebration ceremony to conclude the program
  - ➤ Format 2: Specialists:
    - ✓ Designed for use by prevention specialists from the community who visit the school or organization as experts.
    - ✓ The curriculum is the same as for teachers.
  - ➤ Format 3: Community:
    - ✓ This is designed for outside settings like after-school programs, community and faith community programs, recreational programs, and day camps.
    - ✓ The lessons are the same as classroom lessons but also include:
      - ▪ Nine 60-minute group core meeting lesson plans
      - ▪ Seven 60-minute group booster meeting lesson plans
  - ➤ Booster program:

✓ This is scheduled for one year after initial program
- *Resources:* $1,000–$5,000 for training and materials
- *Settings:* Rural, urban, and suburban
- *Results:*
  - ➢ Decrease in substance use and abuse
  - ➢ Delay in the onset of sexual activity
  - ➢ Reduction in perceived pressure to participate in substance use
  - ➢ Reduced parental tolerance of deviance
  - ➢ Reduction in offers and pressure from peers to use substances
  - ➢ Increased identification and exclusion of negative role models
  - ➢ Increased communication with parents and parental monitoring and supervision
  - ➢ Increased commitment to avoid risky behaviors and set a good example for others
  - ➢ Increased participation in community-focused service projects and commitment to being productive citizens
  - ➢ Increased adoption of positive peer group norms that make substance use, violence, and premature sexual activity unacceptable
  - ➢ Increased student-teacher communication and parent involvement in school

Athletes Training and Learning to Avoid Steroids (ATLAS)

http://nrepp.samhsa.gov/ViewIntervention.aspx?id=77
http://www.colorado.edu/cspv/blueprints/promisingprograms/BPP01.html

- *Goals:* To curb male high school athletes' use of steroids, drugs, and alcohol and to promote healthy exercise and practice programs.
- *Intervention:* Program is integrated into team practice sessions and includes:
  - ➢ 7 to 8 50-minute classroom sessions, covering subjects such as risk factors of steroid use, strength training, sports nutrition, and the skills to refuse steroids and other substances. In addition, nutritional recommendations and false claims of over-the-counter supplements are discussed.
  - ➢ 7 to 8 weight room sessions, providing demonstrations of different weight-lifting techniques, while reinforcing other elements of the classroom curriculum
  - ➢ one-evening informational session for parents
- *Settings:* Schools, recreational centers, and other community organizations with adolescent male athletes
- *Results:*
  - ➢ Less likely to actually use steroids at post-test and 1-year follow-up
  - ➢ Less likely to use alcohol and other drugs (marijuana, amphetamines, and narcotics) at the 1-year follow-up
  - ➢ Less likely to have new occurrences of drinking and driving at the 1-year follow-up

➤ Less likely to intend to use anabolic steroids at post-test
➤ Greater self-reported ability to refuse drug offers from peers at both time periods
➤ Greater knowledge of the effect of steroids and alcohol at both time periods
➤ Heightened perception of coach intolerance to drug use
➤ Improved nutrition behaviors
➤ Enhanced strength training self-efficacy
➤ Greater knowledge of the effects of exercise and sport supplements at post-test and 1-year follow-up
➤ Greater confidence in athletic abilities at post-test and 1-year follow-up
➤ Less likely to believe advertisements for sports supplements and positive steroid use images at both time periods, and sport supplement use lower at 1-year follow-up

Brief Strategic Family Therapy

- *Goals:* To form a therapeutic family alliance, identify patterns that allow for or encourage problematic behavior, and change family interactions that are related to these problem behaviors.
- *Target Outcomes:* To improve youth behavior by eliminating drug use and behaviors associated with it and effect family behavior and practice.
- *Populations:* Children and adolescents from ages 6 to 17 years of age and their families.
- *Problem:* Youth behavior problems, substance abuse, family problems, and problems with peers.
- *Personnel:*
  ➤ Part-time or full-time therapists with a master's degree or bachelor's degree and experience with families
  ➤ Administrative staff is also required to provide support to the families at the most important times.
- *Intervention:*
  ➤ 5–24 weeks
  ➤ Can be implemented in a number of places such as community social services offices, mental health clinics, health agencies, and family clinics.
  ➤ 8–12 weekly 1–1.5 hour sessions
  ➤ Delivered in an office or the family's home:
    ✓ Step 1: Create a positive relationship between counselors and each member of the family in order to form a productive alliance.
    ✓ Step 2: Find the family's strengths and weaknesses and put an emphasis on the behaviors that influence the youth's problematic behavior and those that interfere with the parents' ability to correct them.
    ✓ Step 3: Create a strategy of change that utilizes family strengths to fix problematic family relations. The counselor acts as director of the

conversation and stays plan- and problem-focused.

✓ Step 4: Implement plans that sustain and reinforce family competence, change the meaning of interactions, and change interpersonal boundaries.

- *Resources:* $10,000+ for training, materials, and expenses of up to 5 therapists
- *Settings:* Rural, urban, suburban
- *Results:*
  - ➢ 75% reduction in marijuana use
  - ➢ 42% reduction in conduct problems
  - ➢ 58% reduction in associating with antisocial peers
  - ➢ Improvements in self-concept and self-control
  - ➢ Improvements in family function
  - ➢ Over 75% of families stayed in the program
  - ➢ Increased family participation in therapy
  - ➢ Reduced youth behavior problems and substance abuse
  - ➢ Increased parental involvement and more positive and effective parenting
  - ➢ Improved family cohesiveness, collaboration, and child's bond to the family
  - ➢ Improved family communications, conflict resolution, and problem-solving skills

Creating Lasting Family Connections

http://nrepp.samhsa.gov/ViewIntervention.aspx?id=82
http://www.strengtheningfamilies.org/html/programs_1999/16_CLFC.html

- *Goals:* To strengthen families, reduce and prevent substance abuse and use, and prevent violent behavior in high risk youth.
- *Target Outcomes:* For parents to become more involved in the lives of their children and thus serve as a protective factor against the early involvement of their children in substance use and abuse.
- *Populations:* Youth ages 9–17, their parents, and communities.
- *Problem:* Early substance use and abuse among pre-adolescents and teens and the behaviors that result from such use.
- *Personnel:*
  - ➢ Eight to ten well-respected members of the community should be brought together to assist in recruitment of families
  - ➢ Four facilitators who can work with up to 30 families
- *Intervention:*
  - ➢ 25–52 weeks
  - ➢ 1–3-month training session
  - ➢ 15–18 program sessions with youth
  - ➢ Individual:
    - ✓ After-school substance education
    - ✓ Life and social skills training
  - ➢ Family:

- ✓ Parent education and parenting skill training
  - ▪ How to effectively and positively influence their children
  - ▪ Enhancing parents' skills of dealing with consequences, interventions, substance abuse, and better communication and relationship skills
- ✓ Follow-up services that get families connected to resources
- ➢ Peer:
  - ✓ Peer-resistance education
- • *Settings:* Rural, urban, and suburban
- • *Resources:* $1,000–$5,000 for training and materials
- • *Results:*
  - ➢ Improved parental knowledge of and changed beliefs about substance abuse
  - ➢ Increased parental and youth involvement in setting rules about substance use
  - ➢ Increased use of community services by families, especially when problems arise

Early Risers: Skills for Success

http://nrepp.samhsa.gov/ViewIntervention.aspx?id=137

- • *Goals:* To target children at high risk for conduct problems early through comprehensive and continuing intervention.
- • *Target Outcomes:* Higher academic achievement in participants, better social skills and friend selection, and less aggression in children and better parenting skills.
- • *Populations:*
  - ➢ Youth ages 6–12
  - ➢ Parents of participants
- • *Problem:* Children at high risk for antisocial and aggressive behavior and substance abuse.
- • *Personnel:*
  - ➢ One family advocate for every 25 families
  - ➢ 3–5 day training course needed
- • *Intervention:*
  - ➢ Lasts 2–3 school years
  - ➢ Individual:
    - ✓ Life and social skills training
  - ➢ Family:
    - ✓ Home visits
    - ✓ Parent education and parenting training
    - ✓ Family education sessions to improve family interaction
  - ➢ Peer:
    - ✓ Peer resistance education
    - ✓ Reinforcing negative attitudes about sexual permissiveness
  - ➢ School:
    - ✓ Mentoring

    ✓ Tutoring
- ➢ Core component: Part of the program that takes place in school and summer school, and deals with social and parenting skills and parent education.
- ➢ Flex component: Part of the program for family empowerment, preservation, and resource allocation. Parents and children establish goals for the year and are given access to a variety of resources that they can use to help meet those goals.
- *Settings:* Rural and urban
- *Resources:*
  - ➢ $1,200–$2,000 per child
  - ➢ 3–5-day training program costs $5,000
- *Results:*
  - ➢ Improvement in academic achievement
  - ➢ Significant reductions in behavior problems
  - ➢ Improvements in social skills, social adaptability, and leadership following 3 years of the program
  - ➢ After 4 years of the program participants had more leadership skills, better social etiquette, and chose less aggressive friends with more positive friendship qualities.
  - ➢ Parents showed more investment in their children, less personal distress, and improved disciplined techniques with their children.

Families and Schools Together (FAST)

http://nrepp.samhsa.gov/ViewIntervention.aspx?id=30
http://familiesandschools.org/

- *Goals:* To reduce anxiety and aggression and increase social skills and attention spans in children, to increase family functioning, and to reduce substance use.
- *Target Outcomes:* A reduction in family substance use and child aggression, and an increase in school success for the child.
- *Populations:*
  - ➢ Children ages 5–14
  - ➢ Parents/families of children
- *Problem:* Children's behavioral problems and family dysfunction.
- *Personnel:*
  - ➢ Half-time coordinator
  - ➢ School and parent representative
  - ➢ Two community agency representatives
- *Intervention:*
  - ➢ 1–3 years
  - ➢ Families are offered incentives to join such as food, childcare, fun activities, and transportation.
  - ➢ Sessions involve several families and allow for group and for one-on-one

activities between parents and children.
- ➢ Individual:
  - ✓ After-school substance education
  - ✓ Life and social skills training
- ➢ Family:
  - ✓ Home visits
  - ✓ Parent education and skills training
- ➢ Peer:
  - ✓ Alternative and recreational activities
  - ✓ Classroom and peer support groups reinforcing negative attitudes about sexual permissiveness
  - ✓ Peer resistance education
- *Settings:* Rural, urban, suburban
- *Resources:* $5,000–$10,000 for training and staff salaries
- *Results:*
  - ➢ Decreased aggression and family conflict
  - ➢ Decreased social isolation
  - ➢ Decreased anxiety and attention span problems
  - ➢ Increased social skills, improved academic achievement
  - ➢ Improved communication between family members
  - ➢ Increased respect for family authority
  - ➢ 33% of parents self-referred to substance abuse treatment and mental health counseling
  - ➢ 44% of parents returned to pursue adult education
  - ➢ 10% of parents became community leaders
  - ➢ 86% of parents reported ongoing friendships
  - ➢ 80% of parents who attended one meeting completed the 8-week program

Leadership and Resiliency Program

http://www.promisingpractices.net/program.asp?programid=201

- *Goals:* To prevent teenagers' involvement in substance abuse and violence, and to get them involved in their communities and out-of-school activities.
- *Target Outcomes:* To reduce and prevent teenagers' use and abuse of substances and to reduce and prevent violent behavior.
- *Populations:* 14–19-year-olds
- *Problem:* Teenagers' use of substances and violent behavior.
- *Intervention:*
  - ➢ 1–3 years
  - ➢ Individual:
    - ✓ After-school substance use education
    - ✓ Community service
    - ✓ Life and social skills training

- ➤ Peer:
  - ✓ Alternative recreational activities
  - ✓ Peer resistance education
- ➤ School:
  - ✓ Classroom substance education
  - ✓ Classroom-based skills development
  - ✓ Mentoring/tutoring
- ➤ Community:
  - ✓ Establishment of supervised youth recreational and cultural programs
- *Settings:* Rural, urban, suburban
- *Resources:*
  - ➤ $5,000–$10,000 for:
    - ✓ Consultation
    - ✓ Materials
    - ✓ Training
    - ✓ Program supplies
- *Results:*
  - ➤ 65%–70% reduction in negative behavioral incidents
  - ➤ 75% reduction in school suspensions
  - ➤ 47% reduction in juvenile arrests
  - ➤ Average increase of 0.8 in GPA
  - ➤ 60%–70% increase in school attendance
  - ➤ 100% high school graduation rates
  - ➤ Increased sense of school bonding
  - ➤ High percentage of students became employed or began post-secondary education

Multidimensional Family Therapy (MDFT)

http://nrepp.samhsa.gov/ViewIntervention.aspx?id=16
http://www.strengtheningfamilies.org/html/programs_1999/10_MDFT.html

- *Goals:* To reduce conduct disorders and delinquency in order to help substance-abusing adolescents and those at risk of abuse through family therapy.
- *Target Outcomes:* A reduction in substance abuse, more family involvement and support, and a reduction in problem and risky behaviors.
- *Populations:*
  - ➤ Substance-abusing adolescents
  - ➤ Families of substance abusers
  - ➤ Those at risk for substance abuse
- *Problem:* Substance abuse and behavioral problems.
- *Intervention:*
  - ➤ 4–6 months
  - ➤ Individual:

   ✓ Lessons to deal with youth's current difficulties with school, family, the law, and relationships
   ✓ Enhanced motivation
➢ Peer:
   ✓ Youth's peer group is assessed and the youth is helped to see the danger in having friends who are drug users.
➢ Family:
   ✓ Family sessions, parent-only sessions, and youth-only sessions to address everyday events in the family and family relationships and how to improve them
   ✓ Important past events that are still problematic are addressed
➢ Community:
   ✓ The family is helped to be more aware of the dangers in their community and the resources available to them.
   ✓ The youth are involved in a service in the community that will interest them and will help them develop the skills that they need to develop healthy behaviors
   ✓ Therapists help advocate for the youth in their school and help the parents become involved
   ✓ Therapists work with parents to develop parenting skills and help them get in touch with services that may help them
- *Settings:* Urban, suburban
- *Resources:* $50,000 for budget, material, and training costs
- *Results:*
   ➢ 41%–66% reduction in substance abuse from beginning of program, gains lasted up to 1 year after program
   ➢ At 1 year:
      ✓ 93% of youth reported no substance-related problems
      ✓ 64%–93% reported abstinence from alcohol and drug use
   ➢ Decreased delinquent behaviors and affiliation with delinquent peers
   ➢ Decreased likelihood of being arrested or placed on probation
   ➢ Decreased family conflict, improved parenting practices
   ➢ Significant decrease in disruptive school behaviors and absence from school
   ➢ 43% receive passing grades at high rates

Parenting Wisely (CD-ROM)

http://nrepp.samhsa.gov/ViewIntervention.aspx?id=35
http://www.familyworksinc.com/

- *Goals:* To increase parental communication and disciplinary skills.
- *Target Outcomes:* To improve children's problem behaviors, parents' knowledge, beliefs, and behaviors, and sense of competence.
- *Populations:* Infants–17-year-olds.

- *Problem:* At-risk or exhibiting behavior problems such as substance abuse, delinquency, and dropping out of school.
- *Intervention:* Nine sessions for a total of 2–3 hours. Parents also receive workbooks with program content and exercises to promote skill building.
- *Settings:* Urban, rural, suburban
- *Resources:* $659, plus $6.75–$9 for additional parent workbooks
- *Results:*
  ➢ Significant improvement on the Eyberg Child Behavior Inventory, compared with children of control group parents. Children also showed a significant decrease in negative behaviors as measured by the Parent Daily Report.

Positive Action

http://nrepp.samhsa.gov/ViewIntervention.aspx?id=78
http://www.positiveaction.net/

- *Goals:* To improve children's academic achievement and their behavior through positive actions and behaviors.
- *Target Outcomes:* A reduction in youth substance use and increase in students' academic achievement and social and emotional competence.
- *Populations:* 5–18-year-olds
- *Problem:* Problem behaviors, substance use, and poor academic achievement.
- *Intervention:*
  ➢ Up to 12 years
  ➢ Elementary school:
    ✓ 140 15-minute lessons taught 4 days a week
  ➢ Middle school:
    ✓ 139 lessons taught 4–5 days a week in advisory sessions or homeroom
  ➢ High school:
    ✓ Part 1: lessons for positive living
    ✓ Part 2: a 44-act play in a variety of settings, virtual reality survivor game
    ✓ Part 3: interactive, hands-on activities and projects
    ✓ Part 4: peer mentoring, teaching, role playing
  ➢ Individual:
    ✓ After-school, peer-led substance education
    ✓ Life/social skills training
  ➢ Family:
    ✓ Parent education and parenting skills training
  ➢ Peer:
    ✓ Peer-resistance training
  ➢ School:
    ✓ School change programs to improve parent involvement
    ✓ Improved classroom management or instructional style
    ✓ Improved student commitment to school community

> Community:
  ✓ Multi-agency activities and collaboration
- *Settings:* Rural, urban, and suburban
- *Resources:* $10,000 for training and materials
- *Results:*
  > 71% fewer incidents of substance use in middle schools with a high proportion of program graduates from elementary school
  > Southeastern middle schools: 70% fewer incidents of violence, 60% less disruptive and disrespectful behaviors, 52% less property crime, and 75% less absenteeism
  > Southeastern high schools: 50% fewer incidents of violence, 63% less sexually-related problem behaviors, 28% less disruptive and disrespectful behaviors, 57% fewer incidents of falsifying records, 25% fewer out-of-school suspensions, 30% fewer in-school suspensions, 12% less absenteeism, and 37% lower drop-out rate
  > Nevada: 85% fewer violent incidents per 100 students and 4.5% lower absenteeism
  > Southeastern district: 21% fewer violence-related incidents and 8% fewer suspensions from school

Project ACHIEVE

http://nrepp.samhsa.gov/ViewIntervention.aspx?id=70
http://www.projectachieve.info/

- *Goals:* To improve school performance, school safety, attitudes, and parental involvement to reduce student substance abuse and aggressive behavior.
- *Target Outcomes:* Higher performance in social skills, academic achievement, and problem and conflict resolution.
- *Populations:* 3–14-year-olds
- *Problem:* Poor academic achievement, and aggressive and violent behavior.
- *Personnel:* Full-time, paid staff
- *Intervention:*
  > 3-year program
  > Individual:
    ✓ Life and social skills training
  > Family:
    ✓ Parent education and parenting skills
    ✓ Increased communication between parent and child and between parent and teacher
  > Peer:
    ✓ Peer resistance education
  > School:
    ✓ Classroom substance education

✓ Classroom-based skills development
✓ Programs to improve parental involvement
✓ Improved student participation and school bonding
➢ Community:
  ✓ Multi-agency activities and collaboration
➢ Program Steps:
  1. Strategic Planning and Organizational Analysis and Development
  2. Referral Question Consultation Problem-Solving Process
  3. Effective Classroom and School Processes/Staff Development
  4. Instructional Consultation and Curriculum-Based Assessment
  5. Social Skills, Behavioral Consultation, and Behavioral Interventions
  6. Parent Training, Tutoring, and Support
  7. Research, Data Management, and Accountability
- *Settings:* Rural, urban, suburban, tribal reservations
- *Resources:* $5,000–$10,000 for training and materials
- *Results:*
  ➢ 16% decrease in overall referrals to the principal
  ➢ 29% decrease in out-of-school suspensions
  ➢ 47% grade retention
  ➢ 61% decrease in special education referrals
  ➢ 26% decrease in school bus discipline referrals
  ➢ 33% decrease in special education placements
- *Program Benefits:*
  ➢ Maximize student academic achievement
  ➢ Create safe and positive school climates
  ➢ Increase and sustain effective classroom instruction
  ➢ Increase and sustain strong parent-school involvement
  ➢ Teaches students social skills and self-management behavior

Project Venture (PV)

http://nrepp.samhsa.gov/ViewIntervention.aspx?id=102
http://niylp.org/projects/Project-Venture-Model-Program-Info.pdf

- *Goals:* To help high-risk youth through classroom-based problem-solving activities, outdoor experiential activities, adventure camps and treks, and community-oriented service learning.
- *Target Outcomes:* Positive self-concept, effective social interaction skills, and community service ethic, internal locus of control, and increased decisionmaking and problem-solving skills.
- *Populations:* High-risk American Indian youth and youth from other ethnic groups.

- *Problem:* Substance abuse and problem behaviors in American Indian youth and youth of other ethnic groups.
- *Intervention:*
  - ➢ 25–52 weeks
  - ➢ 20 1-hour lessons delivered over the course of the school year
  - ➢ Activities:
    - ✓ Team and trust-building exercises, hiking, bicycling, and climbing
  - ➢ Individual:
    - ✓ Classroom curricula designed to motivate pro-health decisions
    - ✓ Culturally appropriate activities and curricula incorporating cultural heritage lessons with activities
    - ✓ Life and social skills training
  - ➢ School:
    - ✓ Classroom-based skills development, life skills training with role play
  - ➢ Peer:
    - ✓ Alternative recreational activities
  - ➢ Family:
    - ✓ Parent education
  - ➢ Community:
    - ✓ Mentoring and community service and substance education
    - ✓ Multiagency activities and collaboration
- *Settings:* Rural, tribal reservations
- *Resources:* $100,000 for budget, training, materials, and more optional materials
- *Results:*
  - ➢ Decrease in substance use for participants' lifetimes
  - ➢ Reductions in past 30-day alcohol and illegal drug use
  - ➢ Decreased depression
  - ➢ Decreased aggressive behavior
  - ➢ Improved internal locus of control
  - ➢ Increased resiliency
  - ➢ Improved school attendance

Reconnecting Youth: A Peer Group Approach to Building Life Skills

http://nrepp.samhsa.gov/ViewIntervention.aspx?id=96
http://www.reconnectingyouth.com/ry/

- *Goals:* To prevent behavioral problems and dropping out of high school, and improve youths' emotional competence.
- *Target Outcomes:* Increased school performance, decreased drug involvement, increased attendance, and reduced emotional distress and behavioral problems.
- *Populations:* Students from grades 9–12
- *Intervention:*

- ➤ 5–24 weeks
- ➤ One semester of daily 50-minute classes on four topics: self-esteem, decision-making, personal control and interpersonal communication
- ➤ Other aspects involved are school bonding activities, parental involvement, and school crisis response
- ➤ Individual:
  - ✓ Life and social skills training
- ➤ Family:
  - ✓ Family sessions to improve family interactions
- ➤ Peer:
  - ✓ Alternative recreational activities
  - ✓ Peer resistance education
- ➤ School:
  - ✓ Classroom substance education
  - ✓ Classroom-based skills development
  - ✓ Mentoring and tutoring
- ➤ Community:
  - ✓ Multiagency activities and collaboration
- *Settings:* Urban, suburban
- *Resources:* $5,000–$10,000 for training and materials
- *Results:*
  - ➤ 54% decrease in hard drug use
  - ➤ Curbed progression of alcohol and other drug use
  - ➤ Decreased suicidal behaviors
  - ➤ Decreased anxiety
  - ➤ Decreased depression and hopelessness
  - ➤ 48% decrease in anger control problems and aggression
  - ➤ 18% improvement in grades in all classes
  - ➤ Decreased high school drop out rate

Responding in Peaceful and Positive Ways (RIPP)

http://www.nrepp.samhsa.gov/ViewIntervention.aspx?id=59
http://www.promisingpractices.net/program.asp?programid=238

- *Goals:* To promote nonviolence in schools and give students other ways of dealing with conflict than with fighting, and to reduce the number of violent occurrences in schools.
- *Target Outcomes:* To lower the number of violent incidents in schools and promote nonviolent behavior.
- *Populations:* Middle school and junior high students from grades 6–9.
- *Problem:* Violence in schools.
- *Intervention:*
  - ➤ Delivered over 3 years

- ➢ 6th grade: 25 weekly 50-minute lessons as well as peer mediation group
- ➢ 7th and 8th grade: 12 50-minute lessons over the course of the year. More peer mediation.
- ➢ Curriculum includes: Team-building activities, social and cognitive problem solving, repetition and mental rehearsal, relaxation techniques, small group work, specific skills for preventing violence, role playing, and peer mediation.
- ➢ Individual:
  - ✓ Training for expectations of nonviolence and positive behaviors and achievement
  - ✓ Development of self-management skills
- ➢ Peer:
  - ✓ Mediation training and practice
- ➢ School:
  - ✓ In-class violence prevention lessons
- *Settings:* Rural, urban, suburban
- *Resources:*
  - ➢ $1,000–$5,000 for training and materials
  - ➢ A 5-day training session is necessary
- *Results:*
  - ➢ Decreased frequency of drug abuse
  - ➢ Decreased peer pressure to use drugs
  - ➢ Decreased violations of disciplinary code for violent behavior
  - ➢ Increased peer support for positive behavior
  - ➢ Increased use of violence prevention resources
  - ➢ Increased student and staff reports of improved quality of life
  - ➢ Increased use of peer mediation programs
  - ➢ Fewer in-school suspensions

SAFEChildren

http://www.nrepp.samhsa.gov/ViewIntervention.aspx?id=40
http://www.childtrends.org/Lifecourse/programs/SafeChildren.htm

- *Goals:* To help young children make a successful transition to elementary school and create a solid base for the future.
- *Target Outcomes:* Reductions in problem behaviors and a strong school and community for young children in at-risk areas.
- *Populations:*
  - ➢ Children ages 5–6
  - ➢ Parents
- *Problem:* Young children at risk for future problems.
- *Intervention:*
  - ➢ 5–24 weeks
  - ➢ 20 weeks of family group sessions lasting 2–2.5 hours

> Thirty 30-minute tutoring sessions, 2–3 times a week
> Individual:
  ✓ Designed to be culturally sensitive
  ✓ Builds social and personal skills
> Family:
  ✓ Helps develop bonds among parents in the program
  ✓ Develops parenting skills
  ✓ Task-oriented family sessions to improve family/social interaction
> School:
  ✓ Helps youths keep skills through booster sessions
  ✓ Involves parents in school-based approaches
> Community:
  ✓ Education to change societal norms and expectations regarding school and academic achievement

- *Setting:* Urban
- *Results:*
  > Improvements in academic achievement
  > Reading scores reached the national averages
  > Parents maintained involvement in child's school life
  > Parents gained more effective parenting skills
  > Higher rates of grade-level achievement and school completion
  > Improved self-regulation in children and social competence in adolescents
  > Decreased substance abuse in adolescents
  > Decreased delinquency and violence during adolescence

Strengthening Families Program (SFP)

http://www.nrepp.samhsa.gov/ViewIntervention.aspx?id=44
http://www.colorado.edu/cspv/blueprints/promisingprograms/BPP18.html
http://strengtheningfamiliesprogram.org/

- *Goals:* To improve family relationships, parenting skills, and youths' social and life skills.
- *Target Outcomes:* Stronger families that act as a deterrent for substance use, improved social skills for youth, and improved problem and conflict resolution skills.
- *Populations:*
  > Youth 6–12 years old
  > Parents and families of participating youths
- *Problem:* Youth substance use, aggressive and antisocial behavior, and lack of parental involvement.
- *Intervention:*
  > 14 sessions of 2 hours
    ✓ First hour focuses on children and parents separately

   ✓ Second hour brings children and parents together so they can practice the skills they learned

➢ Two booster sessions at 6 and then 12 months

➢ 4–14 families at one session

➢ Individual:

   ✓ Life and social skills training

➢ Family:

   ✓ Communication skills

   ✓ Parent education and parenting skills training

➢ Peer:

   ✓ Peer resistance education

   ✓ Social skills and communication

- *Settings:* Rural, urban, suburban, tribal reservations
- *Resources:* $5,000–$10,000 for training and materials
- *Results:*

  ➢ Decreases in family conflict and stress

  ➢ Decreased child depression and aggression

  ➢ Decreased substance use among parents and children

  ➢ Improvements in family environment and parenting skills

  ➢ Increased pro-social behaviors in children

  ➢ At 5-year follow up:

     ✓ 92% of families still used acquired parenting skills

     ✓ 68% still held family meetings

Teaching Students to Be Peacemakers

http://www.nrepp.samhsa.gov/ViewIntervention.aspx?id=64
http://www.childtrends.org/Lifecourse/programs/StudentsPeacemakers.htm

- *Goals:* To teach students constructive ways to deal with conflict and give them conflict resolution skills.
- *Target Outcomes:* Students with skills to prevent conflict and to reduce its negative effects.
- *Populations:*

  ➢ K–9

  ➢ Faculty and staff members

- *Problem:* Violence in schools.
- *Intervention:*

  ➢ Twenty 30-minute lessons:

     ✓ Four lessons on the nature of conflict and its potential constructive outcomes

     ✓ Eight lessons on how to engage in problem-solving negotiations

     ✓ Eight lessons on how to mediate schoolmates' conflicts

     ✓ Each lesson has two different student mediators

> Individual:
  - ✓ Classroom curricula designed to motivate pro-health decisions and skills; life skill training and values clarification and antiviolence models
> School:
  - ✓ Classroom-based skill development; creating supportive school communities
> Peer:
  - ✓ Two peer mediators are chosen for each lesson, alternating students so each has a turn.
- *Settings:* Rural, urban, suburban
- *Resources:*
  > $5,000–$10,000
  > Training: $1,000 a day for 5 days with one trainer
  > Materials:
    - ✓ Training manual: $32
    - ✓ Student manual: $12
    - ✓ Video: $30
    - ✓ Audio cassette tape: $12
- *Results:*
  > 62% of program students reached ideal problem-solving constructive solution
  > 29% of students viewed conflicts positively
  > 90% of students recalled 100% of negotiation training the next day
  > 75% of students recalled 100% of training a year after the program
  > Program students use conflict resolution strategies in non-classroom and non-school settings
  > Increased academic achievement and long-term retention of academic material
  > Students resolve conflicts without faculty, reducing classroom problems

Too Good for Violence

http://www.nrepp.samhsa.gov/ViewIntervention.aspx?id=54
http://ies.ed.gov/ncee/wwc/reports/character_education/tgfv/
http://www.mendezfoundation.org/too_good.php

- *Goals:* To improve behavior and minimize aggression in K–12 students.
- *Target Outcomes:* To give students the skills to deal with conflict resolution, anger management, respect and effective communication.
- *Populations:* K–12
- *Problem:* Violence in schools.
- *Intervention:*
  > Seven 30–60-minute lessons per grade for K–5
  > Nine 30–45-minute lessons for grades 6–8
  > Fourteen 60-minute lessons for grades 9–12

- ➤ Individual:
  - ✓ Life and social skills training
- ➤ Peer:
  - ✓ Peer resistance education
  - ✓ Peer norms against violence
  - ✓ Peer norms against substance use
- ➤ School:
  - ✓ Classroom-based education
  - ✓ Classroom-based development
- *Settings:* Rural, urban, suburban
- *Resources:* $1,000–$5,000 for budget, training, and material costs
- *Results:*
  - ➤ Improvements in emotional competence
  - ➤ Improvements in social and conflict resolution skills
  - ➤ Improvements in communication skills
  - ➤ More frequent use of personal and social skills
  - ➤ More pro-social behavior
  - ➤ Increase in negative attitude toward drugs and violence
  - ➤ Improved perceived peer norms
  - ➤ Improved peer disapproval of substance use and knowledge of its harm
  - ➤ Improved emotional competency and self-efficacy
  - ➤ Improved goal setting and decisionmaking skills
  - ➤ 45%–58% reduction in substance use

References

Amen, D., Jellen, L., Merves, E., & Lee, R. (1988). Minimizing the impact of deployment separation on military children: Stages, current preventative efforts and system recommendations. *Military Medicine, 153*(9), 441–446.

Baker, A. (2008). *Life in the U.S. armed forces: (Not) just another job.* Westport, CT: Praeger Security International.

Bradshaw, C. P., Sudhinaraset, M., Mmari, K., & Blum, R. (2010). School transitions among military adolescents: A qualitative study of stress and coping. *School Psychology Review, 39*(1), 84–105.

Burkam, D. T., Lee, V. E., & Dwyer, J. (2009, June 29–30). School mobility in the early elementary grades: Frequency and impact from nationally representative data. Prepared for the workshop on the Impact of Mobility and Change on the Lives of Young Children, Schools, and Neighborhoods, Washington, DC.

Center for Mental Health in Schools at UCLA. (2007). *Welcoming and involving new students and families.* Los Angeles: Author.

Chartrand, M. M., Frank, D. A., White, L. F., & Shope, T. R. (2008). Effect of parents' wartime deployment on the behavior of young children in military families. *Journal of Pediatric Adolescent Medicine, 162*(11), 1009–1014.

Council of State Governments. (2008). Interstate compact on educational opportunity for military children: Legislative resource kit [PDF document]. Available at http://www.csg.org/programs/policyprograms/NCIC/MIC3ResourcesandPublications.aspx

Exum, H. A., Coll, J. E., & Weiss, E. L. (2011). *A civilian primer for counseling military veterans* (2nd ed.). Deer Park, NY: Linus Publications.

Figley, C. R. (1993). Weathering the storm at home: War-related family stress and coping. In F. W. Kaslow (Ed.), *The military family in peace and war* (pp. 163–172). New York: Springer.

Flake, E. M., Davis, B. E., Johnson, P. L., & Middleton, L. S. (2009). The psychosocial effects of deployment on military children. *Journal of Developmental and Behavioral Pediatrics, 30*(4), 271–278.

Gorman, G. H., Eide, M., & Hisle-Gorman, E. (2010). Wartime military deployment and increased pediatric mental health and behavioral complaints. *Pediatrics, 126*(6), 1058–1066.

Gruman, D. H., Harachi, T. W., Abbott, R. D., Catalano, R. F., & Fleming, C. B. (2008). Longitudinal effects of student mobility on three dimensions of elementary school engagement. *Child Development,* 79(6), 1833–1852.

Kerbow, D., Azcoitia, C., & Buell, B. (2003). Student mobility and local school improvement in Chicago. *The Journal of Negro Education,* 72(1), 158–164.

Little, R. W. (1971). The military family. In R. Little (Ed.), *Handbook of military institutions* (pp. 247–270). Beverly Hills, CA: Sage.

Mansfield, A., Kaufman, J., Engel, C., & Gaynes, B. (2011). Deployment and mental health diagnoses among children of U.S. Army personnel. *Archives of Pediatrics and Adolescent Medicine* [Advance online publication]. Available at http://archpedi. ama-assn.org/cgi/content/abstract/archpediatrics.2011.123v1

O'Brien, A. M. (2007). The effect of mobility on the academic achievement of military dependent children and their civilian peers. Peabody College for Teachers of Vanderbilt University.

Paden, L. B., & Pezor, L. J. (1993). Uniforms and youth: The military child and his or her family. In F. W. Kaslow (Ed.), *The military family in peace and war* (pp. 3–24). New York: Springer.

Richardson, A., Chandra, A., Martin, L., Setodji, C. M., Hallmark, B. W., Campbell, N. F., Hawkins, S., & Grady, P. (2011). *Effects of soldiers' deployment on children's academic performance and behavioral health.* Santa Monica, CA: RAND.

Segal, M. W. (1989). The nature of work and family linkages: A theoretical perspective. In G. L. Bowen & D. K. Orthner (Eds.), *The organization family: Work and family linkages in the U.S. military* (pp. 3–36). New York: Praeger.

Smrekar, C. E., & Owens, D. E. (2003). "It's a way of life for us": High mobility and high achievement in department of defense schools. *The Journal of Negro Education,* 72(1), 165–177.

U.S. Government Accountability Office. (2010, December). Many challenges arise in educating students who change schools frequently (Publication No. GAO-11-40). Available at the GAO Reports Main Page via GPO Access database: http://www.gpoaccess.gov/gaoreports/index.html

Wood, D., Halfon, N., Scarlata, D., Newacheck, P., & Nessim, S. (1993). Impact of family relocation on children's growth, development, school function, and behavior. *Journal of the American Medical Association,* 270(11), 1334–1338.

Index

About the Authors

Ron Avi Astor, Ph.D., is the Richard M. and Ann L. Thor Professor of Urban Social Development at the School of Social Work and Rossier School of Education at the University of Southern California. His past work examined the role of the physical, social-organizational, and cultural contexts in schools related to different kinds of school violence (e.g., sexual harassment, bullying, school fights, emotional abuse, weapon use, teacher/child violence). Most recently, his research has examined supportive school climates in military-connected schools.

Linda Jacobson is the editor and writer for the Building Capacity project in the School of Social Work at the University of Southern California. She is a longtime national education reporter and has specialized in writing about early childhood education, state policy, teaching issues, and education research.

Rami Benbenishty, Ph.D., is a professor at Luis and Gaby Wiesfeld School of Social Work of Bar Ilan University and the head of research and evaluation at Haruv Institute. His past research includes numerous published studies on school violence and children, youth at risk, and the implementation of a large-scale school violence prevention model in Israel. Dr. Benbenishty is also an advocate of children's rights and serves on numerous public committees addressing children's needs and rights.

Hazel R. Atuel, Ph.D., is a research assistant professor and project manager of the Building Capacity Consortium. She is a social psychologist and program evaluator, and has expertise in the areas of health disparities, social identities, stereotyping, prejudice, and discrimination. She has managed several large-scale, federally funded projects, including San Diego Unified School District's Safe Schools/Healthy Students initiative and the San Diego Navy Experiment, funded by the Department of Defense in collaboration with the National Institute of Mental Health.

Tamika Gilreath, Ph.D., is an assistant professor in the School of Social Work at the University of Southern California. She has worked on several projects related to substance use including biomedical studies of smoking patterns and performing secondary data analyses of the correlates of smoking among African American youth and adult samples. Her primary research interests include health disparities and patterns of co-morbidity of substance use, and poor mental health among African American youth.

Marleen Wong, Ph.D., is a clinical professor and assistant dean for Field Education in the University of Southern California, School of Social Work. She has been called the "architect of school safety programs," for her work in developing mental health recovery programs, crisis, and disaster training for school districts and law enforcement in the United States, Canada, Israel, and Asia. Formerly, she served as the director of crisis counseling and intervention services for the Los Angeles Unified School District.

Kris M. Tunac De Pedro, Ed.M., is a Ph.D. candidate at the Rossier School of Education, University of Southern California. His research interests include school climate, data-driven decisionmaking, the use of epidemiological research methods in educational research, and military-connected schools.

Monica Christina Esqueda is a Ph.D. student at the Rossier School of Education at the University of Southern California. Her research interests include emerging student populations, student experiences, and the impact of national-, state-, and local-level policies on student experiences.

Joey Nuñez Estrada Jr., Ph.D., is an assistant professor at the College of Education, San Diego State University. His research interests include school violence, street gang culture, school-based intervention, resiliency, and youth empowerment. His work has been published in major academic journals and he has presented his research at various conferences. He is currently conducting research on the risk and protective factors for gang-involved youth within school communities.